30 ANIMALS
THAT SHARE OUR
WORLD

EDITED BY JEAN REYNOLDS

An INK Nonfiction Minute Book

SEA
GRASS

Brimming with creative inspiration, how-to projects, and useful information to enrich your everyday life, Quarto Knows is a favorite destination for those pursuing their interests and passions. Visit our site and dig deeper with our books into your area of interest: Quarto Creates, Quarto Cooks, Quarto Homes, Quarto Lives, Quarto Drives, Quarto Explores, Quarto Gifts, or Quarto Kids.

Inspiring | Educating | Creating | Entertaining

First published in 2018 by Seagrass Press, an imprint of The Quarto Group.
6 Orchard Road, Suite 100, Lake Forest, CA 92630, USA.
T (949) 380-7510 **F** (949) 380-7575 **www.QuartoKnows.com**

Seagrass Press titles are also available at discount for retail, wholesale, promotional, and bulk purchase. For details, contact the Special Sales Manager by email at specialsales@quarto.com or by mail at The Quarto Group, Attn: Special Sales Manager, 401 Second Avenue North, Suite 310, Minneapolis, MN 55401 USA.

ISBN: 978-1-63322-500-8

Digital edition published in 2018
ISBN: 978-1-63322-501-5

Illustrations by Natasha Hellegouarch
Interior design by Marc Cheshire

Printed in China
10 9 8 7 6 5 4 3 2 1

MIX
Paper from
responsible sources
FSC® C101537

Don't miss the first book in this series: *30 People Who Changed the World*

CONTENTS

Introduction

BY JEAN REYNOLDS

Dear Readers,

You've probably met a lot of animals. In fact, you might even live with one or more of them. And, no doubt you've visited a zoo now and then and encountered some interesting and exotic animals. But I can practically guarantee that you'll still be surprised and fascinated by little-known habits and quirky stories of the animals our Nonfiction Minute authors have chosen to introduce you to, including:

- Skunks have a bad rep and for good reason. But did you know that they are one of the politest and nicest animals in the animal kingdom? Before they release their foul spray, they will always warn you—not once, not twice, but three times. How considerate.
- What color is a polar bear? Wrong! Polar bear skin is actually black. Find out why you picked the wrong answer.
- You probably know what the biggest vertebrate in the world is, but do you have any idea what the smallest is? No, insects don't count. They don't have backbones.
- So you think you know dogs and cats pretty well? They can still surprise you. You're about to meet a

commuting cat who, all on his own, takes a daily roundtrip train ride to view a penguin exhibit. Or, if you're a dog person, you'll feel very proud to meet the dog who was promoted to the rank of Sergeant in the US Armed Forces.

- And don't be so sure you know a lot about the little creepy crawlies you see every day. If you knew them well, you'd have noticed that spiders have smelly feet and daddy longlegs have toxic armpits.

So dive into *30 Animals that Share Our World* and enjoy getting the inside scoop on a variety of interesting creatures. The added bonus is that you'll be reading the work of a dozen talented nonfiction writers, all award-winning authors of books for kids and young adults. While learning more about these animals, you might even pick up some pointers about how to go about writing enjoyable nonfiction.

Enjoy every minute,

Jean Reynolds
Editor
The Nonfiction Minute
nonfictionminute.org

The Invasion of the Wolf Spiders

BY TRISH MARX

When I was about 10 years old, I lived in a small town on a prairie. I had to walk to and from school each day taking a shortcut through our dark, crowded garage. This was fine until the spiders set up home in each corner of the garage-door opening. They spun huge blobs of flimsy webs which hung there ready to drop on my head or down my back. I ran under them to the safety of the alley. They feasted on Minnesota's mosquitos, growing to what I imagined to be tennis-

Wolf spider preying on a grasshopper

Would you like this fellow waiting for you in your garage?

ball-sized bodies with red and yellow stripes, long and thick hairy legs, and large bulb-like eyes. My brother and sister thought they were monsters; we shudder when we remember them.

Actually, they were wolf spiders. Like wolves, they're predators. They lie in wait for prey to come close. Then they chase and pounce on it, stinging it with their venom that dissolves the prey's organs so the spider can suck up the nourishment.

In March of 2012, wolf spiders made news in Wagga Wagga, Australia (a town of 50,000), a few hours south of Sydney, Australia's largest city. Some say due to climate change, it rained much more than usual, causing the usually peaceful river that flowed through the town to flood nearby fields. It flooded the hibernation holes of the wolf spiders, which they had dug a few months earlier in the sunbaked ground, lining their nests with silk, ready for the coming winter. The floodwaters woke up the spiders, which fled for higher ground—bushes, trees, houses, poles . . . any

Does it look like it just snowed in Wagga Wagga? It didn't. It rained, and you're looking at the wolf spider webs spread across the land.

The way wolf spiders carry their eggs is unique. The egg sac, a round silken globe, is attached to the spinnerets at the end of the abdomen, allowing the spider to carry her unborn young with her.

high places. As more than a million spiders ran, they trailed behind "drag lines" of silk that caught the wind, lifting some of them through the air. Countless thin trails of silk covered the bushes and fields, creating a blanket of web, looking like snow. No one had seen anything like it. When I read it about it, I knew instantly that this was the spider that terrorized me as a child. Wolf spiders are found all over the world, including Minnesota and Australia.

I believe that this was a small whisper from the earth about what is happening to it. If this damage in Wagga Wagga was caused by climate change, imagine the invasions and changes that may yet come. The next change could be a shout.

Find Out More

VISIT: izismile.com/2013/11/19/a_terrifying_spider_invasion_in_australia_12_pics_1_gif.html

WATCH: video.dailymail.co.uk/video/bc/rtmp_uds/1418450360/2012/03/07/1418450360_1492942365001_Spider-webs-in-Aus.mp4

In Praise of Vultures

BY STEPHEN SWINBURNE

I really like vultures. Sure, they're ugly and they eat nasty dead things. But those are not necessarily bad characteristics.

First, let's deal with "ugly." Vultures' bald heads are what make them seem ugly to most people. But think about why they're bald. Imagine thrusting your head inside the carcass of a white-tailed deer to reach the meat. A hairy head might capture bits of flesh, blood and gore and you end up with a face full of bacteria and flies. Scientists believe that one reason vultures have evolved featherless heads is to aid in hygiene. A bald head stays clean and any remaining germs or bacteria are baked off by the sun. Also, their bald heads can help with temperature regulation. When the temperature drops, they can tuck their heads down. When it's hot, vultures can extend their neck to expose

The turkey vulture got its name because the adult's bald red head and its dark plumage look similar to that of the male wild turkey.

The two types of vultures are the New World vultures who live in South and North America and the Old World vultures of Europe, Africa, and Asia. The turkey vulture and this black vulture are two of the seven species of New World vultures.

bare skin. Their bald heads work so well that I wrote a poem about them.

Naked Head
It's best to have no feathers,
When you stick your head in guts,
That way you don't go walkin' 'round,
Your noggin dripping schmutz.

Moving on to "eating nasty dead things," the next time you see vultures eating a dead animal on the side of the road, be thankful! That carcass might be dead from rabies or contaminated with other harmful diseases.

Vultures have the amazing ability to consume rotting and diseased flesh and stay healthy. It's all in the stomach. Vultures possess very powerful stomach acids that destroy most bacteria and deadly viruses. In fact, vulture stomach acid is so strong that it can dissolve metal—except if that metal is lead shot. (Many turkey vultures are killed every year by consuming shot that they encounter in dead deer.) Vultures are the world's natural "sanitation workers," helping to stop the spread of disease. I'm so appreciative of the work they do, I even wrote a follow-up poem about eating dead things:

Dead Meat
I like my meat dead,
It's best if it's not moving.
Don't want to see one final twitch,
I prefer it oozing.

The California condor is part of the New World vulture family. This drawing is from Audubon's *The Birds of America*.

Bald heads are not the only way vultures stay clean. They urinate straight down their legs. The uric acid kills bacteria accumulated from walking through carcasses.

So the next time you see a vulture circling in the noonday sky, think about the valuable and important cleanup service this bird provides to us and to the environment. Maybe I'll write a poem about that....

Find Out More

READ: *Vulture: The Private Life of an Unloved Bird* by Katie Fallon

VISIT: kern.audubon.org/tvfacts.htm

WATCH: youtube.com/watch?v=_yllQwGMbi0

Rites and Bites of Passage

BY SARAH ALBEE

Bullet ants can grow to be about an inch (2.5 cm) long, and they are among the world's most venomous insects. They also deliver the most painful sting of any insect, according to J. O. Schmidt. He's an entomologist who's been stung by pretty much every hymenopteran possible and who developed a pain-scale rating that lists the relative pain caused by insects. His ratings go from 0, where the sting is as mild as the little zap you might feel while walking across a carpet in your socks, up to 4, where you might as well just lie down and scream. Bullet ants get

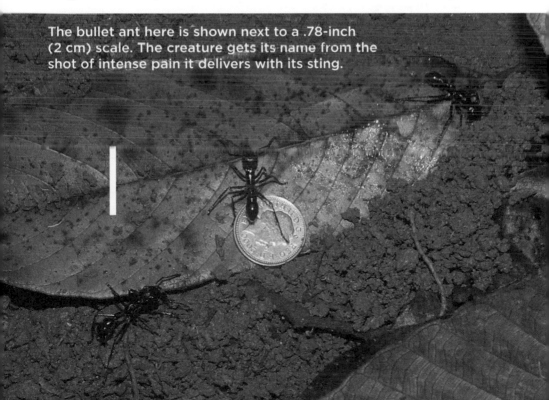

The bullet ant here is shown next to a .78-inch (2 cm) scale. The creature gets its name from the shot of intense pain it delivers with its sting.

Entomologist J. O. Schmidt developed a pain-scale rating that lists the relative pain caused by insect stings.

a 4+. When he later revised his index, he described bullet ant stings as "pure, intense, brilliant pain, like walking over flaming charcoal with a three-inch nail in your heel."

But wait, it gets worse.

The ants have abdominal stridulatory organs. That means they can shriek at you when threatened, which alerts the rest of the group to come boiling up out of the nest to help impale you.

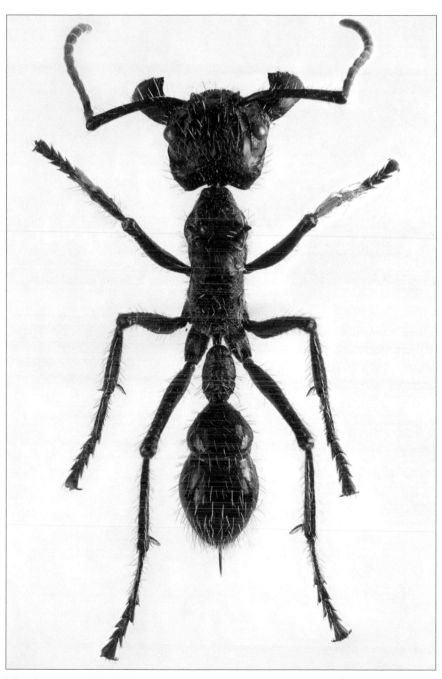

The insect called *Paraponera clavata* is commonly known as a bullet ant. They live mainly in the rain forests of Central America, so you probably don't have to worry about coming into contact with one.

Sateré-Mawé shamans lull a hive of ants into paralysis with smoke and then sew the living ants (stinger end out) into a mitten-like structure made of grass. When the ants regain consciousness, young boys stick their hands into the mitten as a rite of manhood.

There's a tribe of people in Brazil, deep in the Amazon forest, the Sateré-Mawé, who use bullet ants as an initiation rite to manhood. Boys have to slip on gloves that resemble oven mitts. Live bullet ants are woven into these gloves, with the stingers pointing toward the wearer's hands. The boys have to keep the gloves on for ten minutes. Evidently, paralysis of the arms sets in rather quickly, so after the gloves come off, the real pain and convulsions begin, lasting at least twenty-four hours.

Did I mention they also shriek?

FIND OUT MORE:

VISIT: esquire.com/lifestyle/health/a37149/what-feels-like-stung-by-most-painful-insect/

WATCH: youtube.com/watch?v=jIU27rc19wM
youtu.be/tXjHb5QmDV0?t=63

Here Come the Cicadas!

BY LAURENCE PRINGLE

Almost every spring an amazing event happens in parts of the United States. Huge numbers of insects called periodical cicadas emerge from the soil. For a few weeks, they fill the days with loud buzzing calls.

Every summer you can hear the calls of some kinds of cicadas, but periodical cicadas are different. They exist only in the eastern two-thirds of the United States and are the longest-living insects. Some periodical cicadas live thirteen years; others reach

If you live in the US states of CT, GA, MD, NC, NJ, NY, OK, PA, VA and you missed seeing a 17-year cicada in 2013, you'll have wait until 2030 to see another one. Other US states have different timetables, but all have seventeen-year intervals.

Female cicadas deposit rice-shaped eggs into grooves they make on a tree limb. The tree feeds and shelters the young cicadas, but the process can kill small branches.

Once the egg hatches, the cicada feeds on the tree fluids. When it is ready, it will drop to the ground. There it burrows into the soil and finds plant roots to feed on. Once it reaches the roots, cicadas can stay active underground, tunneling and feeding, for as long as seventeen years before emerging as a nymph.

seventeen years, with nearly all of that time spent underground. Young cicadas, called nymphs, sip water and nutrients from tree roots. The nymphs count the years, probably by sensing seasonal changes in tree sap.

When their countdown ends and soil warms in the spring, millions of cicada nymphs dig out. They climb posts, bushes, and trees, and cling there. Their nymph "skins" split open and adult cicadas wriggle free. Finally, after many years underground, they are out in the sunshine. They can fly, and the buzzing noises of males attract females. It is a noisy and hectic time in their lives. They have just a few weeks to mate and produce the next generation. Once females lay eggs in tree twigs, all of the adults die. Soon after, tiny nymphs hatch from the eggs. They drop to the soil, burrow in, and begin to sip juices from tree roots. The nymphs

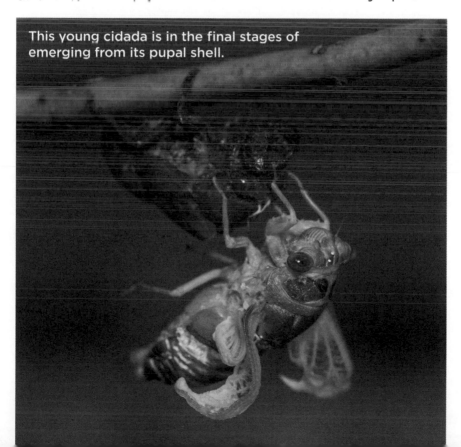

This young cidada is in the final stages of emerging from its pupal shell.

Cicada nymphs emerge after a seventeen-year childhood underground.

grow slowly, counting the years until they will have their own time in the sun.

Nearly every year, one or more populations, called broods, of periodical cicadas emerge. Seventeen-year cicadas live mostly in the Northeast and upper Midwest. Thirteen-year cicadas are most common in the South and lower Midwest. Some broods emerge in parts of just a few states. Some years, a more widespread brood emerges in parts of fifteen states. Notice that I say "parts" of states. These cicadas don't roam around. The nymphs go underground in the same places where their parents emerged. You will find them in one town but not another, in one neighborhood but not another.

Some people call cicadas "locusts," but locusts are a kind of grasshopper that eats plants. Cicadas do not chew on plants. They are harmless, fascinating creatures. And, once in a great while, they give us a rare and awe-inspiring animal spectacle.

FIND OUT MORE

READ: *Cicadas!: Strange and Wonderful* by Laurence Pringle; *The Bizarre Life Cycle of a Cicada* by Greg Roza

VISIT: cicadamania.com

WATCH: youtube.com/watch?v=x71RaI-RxVM

Do Animals Ask for Help?

BY ALINE ALEXANDER NEWMAN

Dogs depend on us for friendship, food, and shelter. But wild animals run from people. They don't turn to humans for help when they need to get out of trouble. Or do they? Until recently, most scientists thought animals could not think through multiple steps to solve problems. They believed only people could do that. But research into animal behavior shows this is not true. At least some animals think through their problems and come up with possible solutions.

Take, for example, a young, wild raven, in Elmsdale,

A desperate koala approaches humans, letting them know he needs liquid.

Nova Scotia. In 2013, Gertie Cleary spied the bird perched on a fence with porcupine quills stuck in its wing and face. Porcupine quills are barbed, like fish hooks, and they really hurt. Cleary slipped on a pair of gloves before approaching the bird. Now you might think the raven would get scared and fly away. Not this

A baby bird in trouble. Has another bird gone for help?

bird. This bird wanted help. It screeched in pain each time Cleary plucked out a quill. But it sat still and let her do it. "When I pulled the one out of his wing," Cleary says, "he fell off the fence I pulled it so hard." Once quill-free, the raven flew away.

A real-life mother goose went a step further. When one of her goslings became tangled in a balloon string, she "called" the cops by pecking on the door of a police cruiser parked nearby. When the curious cops exited their vehicle, she led them straight to her helpless baby.

My family and I also encountered a bird in trouble. We were walking on a nature trail when the bushes suddenly erupted with chirping. We stopped, and the chirping increased.

Looking closely, we found a sparrow stuck on a thistle bush! It was hanging upside down. We felt like heroes when we freed the little creature and watched it fly away.

Birds aren't the only animals that ask for help. In Fairfax, California, a deer approached a police car and stared at the officer inside until he noticed her broken leg. On March 1, 2016, a scorching hot day, in Adelaide, Australia, a thirsty koala begged a group of cyclists for a drink of water. In 2016 on a nature reserve in South Africa, a desperate mother giraffe led a wildlife guide to her injured calf. In every case, kind humans helped.

Maybe someday you will rescue an animal and save a life. Wouldn't that be great?

Find Out More

VISIT: huffingtonpost.com/matt-trezza/seven-times-wild-animals-_b_9277254.html

WATCH: youtube.com/watch?v=7Vj05uXDKYU

A giraffe mother was willing to ask for human help in order to save her baby.

Reading Has Gone to the Dogs

BY DAVID M. SCHWARTZ

A celebrity has just arrived in Mr. Madison's classroom at El Verano Elementary School in Sonoma, California, and the third graders are beside themselves. "Here he is!" they exclaim as the visitor walks through the door.

This special guest has not come to give a lesson or tell a story. He is neither a star athlete nor a movie star. He doesn't play an instrument, sing, dance or perform

Reading relaxes Fenway as well as the reader.

Fenway seems to be paying close attention to this young reader.

magic tricks. His tricks are mostly limited to sit, stay, and shake. He is a dog. His name is Fenway Bark.

The eight-year-old chocolate-colored Labrador Retriever has been coming to El Verano for six years with his owner, Mara Kahn. He has helped hundreds of children become better readers. Fenway is a literacy dog.

"Fenway's job is to listen while you're reading," explains Mara to the class, which is gathered in a circle around her and Fenway.

One of the best ways for children to improve their reading is to read aloud, but reading in front of an audience can be scary. What if Chelsea mispronounces

Animals as well as kids benefit from animal shelter reading sessions.

a word? Or if Alex loses track of where he is on the page? Will everyone laugh? The fear can discourage some children from reading aloud at all.

The solution to this problem is to read to a nonjudgmental audience that doesn't care what you read or how you read it. Read to a dog! When reading to dogs, young readers don't have to worry about saying "whoof" when they meant to say "which." With less anxiety and more confidence, children increase their reading fluency. That's why literacy dogs visit hundreds of schools and libraries as reading buddies for children.

Vanessa sits cross-legged on the rug in Mr. Madison's classroom. She gingerly opens *Strega Nona* by Tomie dePaola. Softly, slowly, she reads about Big Anthony who ignores Strega Nona's instructions not to touch her magical pasta pot. Fenway sits up and looks at Vanessa. He gazes at the floor. Vanessa keeps reading. The pasta starts flowing. Fenway stretches out. Vanessa reads a little louder, a little faster. Pasta floods the town. Fenway licks Vanessa's knee. She giggles and goes back to her book.

Six children got to read to the canine visitor. "It's so cool to read to a dog," said one boy who will get his chance next week. He was already thinking about choosing a doggone good book.

Find Out More

READ: Give it a try yourself. Read aloud to a dog.

VISIT: stories.barkpost.com/discover/dogs-and-child-literacy

WATCH: youtu.be/-EbsPAnfOdg
youtube.com/watch?v=Rve1DukX3Mo

This boy seems much more excited about reading the story than the dog is about listening to it, but it doesn't matter. The boy is happily reading aloud!

The postman butterfly is poisonous and features colorful markings (often red) on its wings as a warning to predators.

Smelling Feet or Smelly Feet?

BY DOROTHY HINSHAW PATENT

Do your feet sometimes smell rotten? Do you wish you could toss out your shoes and start with a new pair? We make jokes about smelly feet, but smell and feet have a very different relationship among some insects.

Take butterflies. Have you ever watched a butterfly flit over a plant, gently touch its feet to a leaf, and then fly on to the next leaf? That butterfly isn't being picky about where to land. It's hunting for the right kind of leaf for laying its eggs. It's "smelling" the leaf with its feet!

Actually, we need to qualify that statement a bit. Some writers will say the insect is "smelling" the leaf while others may write that it's "tasting" the leaf. Smelling and tasting are forms of "chemoreception,"

Male	Female

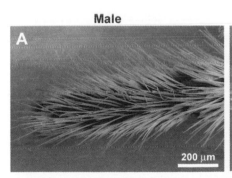

In these photographs taken through a microscope, you can see that the male on the left does not have the sensory sensilla shown (arrow) on the feet of the female butterfly at right.

Postman butterflies do not spend much time or energy collecting nectar. Instead, they collect pollen with their proboscis. Then they agitate the pollen by coiling and uncoiling their proboscis in order to release its nutrients.

or sensing of chemicals. Smell usually refers to sensing from a distance, and tasting generally means actually touching the nerve cells that sense a chemical.

We humans have cells in our noses that send messages to our brains about chemicals in the air. We call that our sense of smell. We have cells on our tongues that sense chemicals dissolved in liquid in our mouths. That's taste.

That butterfly doesn't have a nose, and its mouth is a long tube for sucking nectar from flowers. Its chemoreceptors are elsewhere, like on its feet, around its mouth, and on its antennae. Most butterflies lay their eggs on the plants that their hatched caterpillars will eat. Some species are very specific about what plants their young can feed on. Take the postman butterfly, which lives in Central and South America.

Its caterpillars can only survive on certain species of passionflower vines. Other species are poisonous to their offspring.

The female postman butterfly has dozens of special nerve cells on her feet called "gustatory sensilla." Scientists think that when the butterfly touches gently down on a leaf, these cells can sense chemicals there that would be poisonous to her caterpillars. She avoids laying eggs on those leaves. But when she finds a plant that will nourish her young, she'll alight and lay her eggs.

Now take your shoes off and move your feet around on the floor. The only nerve endings on your feet are ones that sense touch. That's because you have no need to be able to smell the ground you walk on. Imagine how gross it would be if your feet could smell the insides of your socks and shoes. Yuck!

Find Out More

VISIT: agriculture.purdue.edu/agcomm/newscolumns/archives/OSL/1993/January/011493OSL.html

WATCH: youtube.com/watch?v=xiBBm9u2ex4

Postman butterflies have bright color patterns that warn potential predators that the butterflies are distasteful and should be avoided.

This little Brazilian Gold Frog is not little enough to maintain the shared title of the world's smallest frog.

Tiny Frogs Are Big News

BY LAURENCE PRINGLE

Can you name the world's fastest mammal? How about the biggest shark? If you said the cheetah, and the whale shark, you're right! It's safe to say that we will probably never discover faster or bigger animals. However, it is still possible to find small animals that can set new records for being tiny.

Take frogs, for example. For many years, two kinds of frogs were tied for the honor of being the world's smallest. One species, known as the Monte Iberia dwarf frog lives In Cuba. The other is the Brazilian Gold Frog which gets its name from its golden color.

An Amau frog hanging out on a dime.

Because Amau frogs have calls that resemble those made by insects and are camouflaged among leaves on the forest floor, they are difficult to detect and capture.

The two are about the size of a housefly.

Recently, those two little species from Cuba and Brazil lost their title as Earth's smallest frogs, thanks to two scientists from the United States. They were herpetologists (scientists who study amphibians, including salamanders and frogs). In 2009, these scientists were studying frog calls on Papua New

Guinea, a large island nation north of Australia, in the Pacific Ocean.

The scientists were recording frog calls at night. All around, they heard chirping sounds that came from dead leaves on the forest floor. "Probably insects," they thought, but they decided to check. They searched among the leaves but found nothing. Frustrated, they grabbed whole handfuls of leaves and stuffed them into a clear plastic bag. Then they slowly searched through the bag, leaf by leaf. A small frog hopped off one of the leaves!

When I say "small frog," I mean one that can sit on a dime with room to spare. It was just 7.7 millimeters (0.3 inch) long. Although the scientists later discovered another slightly bigger relative, the one they found in the plastic bag is now officially Earth's smallest frog—and Earth's smallest four-footed animal.

These tiny frogs are hard to catch. They can leap thirty times their own length. But the herpetologists managed to catch quite a few, take photos of them, and learn about their lives close up. It wasn't until January 2012 that the scientists announced their discovery. Since this frog was discovered near a village called Amau, it was given the scientific name of Amauensis. Eventually, people may come to call it the Amau frog.

In the world of science, the tiny Amau frogs are very big news.

FIND OUT MORE

READ: *Frogs! Strange and Wonderful* by Laurence Pringle

VISIT: phys.org/news/2012-03-student-world-smallest-frog.html

Stubby's jacket features an official sergeant insignia on the upper left.

Sergeant Stubby

BY CHERYL HARNESS

If you go to the official World War I Museum of the United States, in Kansas City, Missouri, you might see a paving stone that reads:

> *"Sergeant Stubby*
> *Hero Dog of World War I*
> *A Brave Stray"*

And you might say, "Huh?" So here's his story, just for you to know.

In 1917 Connecticut, a terrier puppy strayed onto a Yale University field, where soldiers were training to fight in World War I. There is *much* to say about world-changing WWI. For instance, it began in the late

Sergeant Stubby's paving stone at the Liberty Memorial in Kansas City.

This photo of Stubby wearing his coat of many medals was taken between 1918 and 1921.

summer of 1914 in Europe. On April 6, 1917, the United States joined twenty-three other allied countries, such as Great Britain, in their fight against the Central Powers: Germany, Austria-Hungary, Bulgaria, and the Ottoman Empire.

The puppy quickly learned army life and lots of tricks. Private John R. Conroy adopted the pup he named "Stubby" and tried to sneak him overseas. When Stubby was discovered, he charmed the angry officer by raising his right paw and saluting him!

Stubby and Conroy served in France, by Germany's border, where millions of soldiers fought one another along a 450-mile (724-km) battle line. This was WWI's deadly Western Front. Soon, Stubby was nearly killed by poison gas. Because the attack sensitized his nose, he became a barking, life-saving, put-your-mask-on-early warning device! With his sensitive ears, Stubby could hear a lost or injured man, then go help him. Once, he heard a suspicious-sounding man. Stubby chased and caught a German spy by the seat of his pants! For this, Sergeant Stubby, the official mascot of the 26th Division of the American Expeditionary Forces, became the first dog ever promoted by the US Armed Forces.

WWI ended when the victorious Allies made their enemies agree to an Armistice: As of 11 a.m. November 11, 1918, the fighting would stop.

For his brave actions, battle-scarred Sgt. Stubby was WWI's most decorated dog. Even the top US officer, General John J. Pershing himself, gave him a medal! How did Stubby wear his awards? They were attached to his soft leather blanket, made by

Stubby proudly wore an American flag on his harness in a parade.

Sgt. Stubby: An American Hero is a computer-animated feature film based on the incredible true story of America's most decorated dog.

grateful Frenchwomen. Stubby met three Presidents (Wilson, Harding, and Coolidge). In America, Stubby was in many victory parades, and he appeared at Georgetown University football games, too, as their team mascot. (Conroy studied law there.)

Faithful Sgt. Stubby was about ten years old when he passed away in Conroy's arms on March 16, 1926. His obituary was printed in the *New York Times*. You can visit Stubby (his preserved remains anyway), in Washington, D.C., at the Smithsonian Museum of American History.

FIND OUT MORE

READ: *Stubby the War Dog: The True Story of World War I's Bravest Dog* by Ann Bausum

VISIT: amhistory.si.edu/militaryhistory/collection/object.asp?ID=15

WATCH: youtube.com/watch?v=9esx_qre9n4
youtube.com/watch?v=cQe_7NNoA-0

The Way Polar Bears Stay Warm is Cool

BY VICKI COBB

Polar bears are built to withstand some of the coldest temperatures on the planet. Their brown and black bear cousins avoid the winter cold by digging dens and sleeping. With the exception of pregnant females, polar bears spend the arctic winter outside where temperatures reach zero degrees Fahrenheit (-18° C) and it is windy. That's too cold for humans. You could go outside, but only for only a few minutes with every part of your body completely covered. And if you didn't wear goggles, your eyelashes would freeze and break off if you touched them.

Polar bears are warm-blooded like us humans with

The polar bears' white appearance serves as ideal camouflage in a snow-covered environment.

Polar bears feed mainly on seals. Depending upon their location, they also scavenge on carcasses of beluga whales, walruses, narwhals, and bowhead whales.

a body temperature of about 98°F (37°C). But they are invisible to night-vision goggles that pick up the infrared rays that warm-blooded creatures, including humans, give off. Why? Nature has given polar bears enough insulation to prevent body heat from escaping. They are toasty warm and comfortable in the frigid arctic.

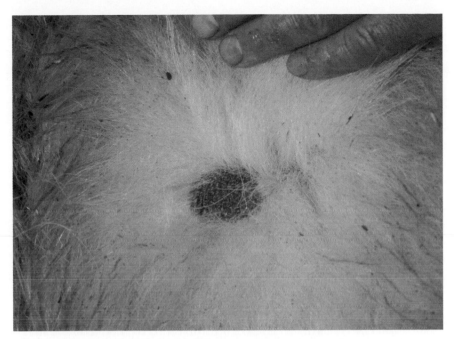

A rare peek under the beautiful white polar bear fur.

Their heat insulation is in several layers. Under their skin, there is a 4-inch (10.6-cm) layer of fat. Next to the skin is a dense layer of woolly fur that also keeps heat in. The fur you see is a thick layer of long, colorless guard hairs that shed water quickly after a swim. They are stiff, transparent, and hollow. In the arctic sunlight, the hairs act like mirrors and reflect white light, which acts as camouflage against the snow so the bears are not seen by their prey. Polar bear skin is actually black, so that it can absorb the invisible warm infrared rays of the sun and the bear's own body heat, both of which are reflected back by the guard hairs.

Most warm-blooded animals raise their body temperatures through exercise. Polar bears hunt seals, which they don't often chase. They prefer to sit at the edge of an ice floe and wait for dinner to arrive. At best, they'll lumber after a seal at 4.5 miles (7.25 km) an hour, raising their body heat to 100°F (38°C). When

If you look very closely at the fur around the polar bear's neck, you will get a rare glimpse of the black skin showing through.

that happens, they go for a swim to cool off.

Cold won't kill off the polar bears, but global warming can. As polar ice disappears, so does the hunting ground for seals. Not so cool!

Find Out More

READ: *Animal Predators: Polar Bears* by Sandra Markle

VISIT: polarbearsinternational.org

WATCH: vimeo.com/156505076
youtube.com/watch?v=L8u8ta1gdgU

Alligator Smiles

BY STEPHEN SWINBURNE

Alligators are one of the world's most feared predators. With rows of dagger-sharp teeth, a muscled reptilian body, a dinosaur face and eyes, alligators frighten yet fascinate people. Scientists are working hard to understand this modern-day reptile.

Dr. Daphne Soares, at the time a biology professor at the University of Maryland, was intrigued by the hunting ability of the alligator. She knew that alligators have keen eyesight and excellent hearing, but there was something else that made them such efficient predators—the king of the swamp. Careful focus on the dark bumps all over the animal's upper and lower jaws led her to conclude that these bumps "were very sensitive tactile organs that can detect ripples in the water." The ability to feel waves or ripples is one of the many features that make the alligator an excellent

Alligators have a long, rounded snout that has upward facing nostrils at the end; this allows the alligator to breathe while the rest of its body is underwater.

An American Alligator in captivity at the Columbus Zoo, Powell, Ohio. Exceptionally large males can weigh nearly half a ton or 1,000 pounds (454 kilograms).

A smiling American Alligator displays the bumps around its upper and lower jaws.

predator. Once the alligator detects ripples, it swims swiftly and silently in the direction of the prey.

Alligators are carnivores. They seize and hold their prey with sharp teeth. Small quarry, such as fish and ducks, are swallowed whole. Larger victims are shaken apart into smaller, bite-size pieces. Gators have between 74 and 80 teeth in their jaws at a time. When their teeth get worn down, they are replaced with new ones. Imagine that! No need for a dentist. Alligators can go through 2,000 to 3,000 teeth in a lifetime.

When it comes to snagging a meal, the alligator is all carnivore with a mouth full of awesome teeth. But the female alligator also uses her jaws to be an awesome mom. She lays 35 to 50 eggs, each about twice the size of a chicken egg. When the baby alligators are ready, the mother helps her babies to break out of their shells.

Newly hatched alligators are six to eight inches (15 to 20 cms) long. Mother gathers them up in her

A baby alligator is safe in its mother's mouth.

fearsome mouth and carries them to the safety of shallow water. Their mom will stay with them and safeguard them from predators, such as great blue herons and raccoons.

Alligators are a rare success story of an endangered species saved from the brink of extinction. As late as 1950s, alligators were hunted for meat and hide. They were placed on the Endangered Species list in 1967, and now thrive in the freshwater swamps and wetlands of the southeastern United States.

Find Out More

READ: *American Alligators: Freshwater Survivors* (America's Animal Comebacks) by Aaron Feigenbaum

VISIT: myfwc.com/wildlifehabitats/managed/alligator/education/

WATCH: youtube.com/watch?v=RQpj8tpxPcM

Animals in Space

BY ROXIE MUNRO

You're probably too young to remember Laika, a stray dog from the Moscow streets, who was famous for becoming the first animal to orbit the earth. That was way back in 1957, when space exploration was taking off, and Russia was ahead of the game.

Laika wasn't the first animal to fly. When the first free-flying hot-air balloon ever to carry living creatures was launched at Louis XVI's magnificent chateau in Versailles, France, in 1783, its passengers were a sheep, a duck, and a rooster.

Some 130,000 people watched as the multicolored

Antonio Carnicero, *Ascent of the Monsieur Bouclé's Montgolfier Balloon in the Gardens of Aranjuez*, 1784, Oil on Canvas, Prado Museum, Madrid.

The local populous was awed by the newfangled balloon vehicle and amazed by its passengers!

balloon filled with hot air stirred and rose, carrying a basket with the animals. The king was there, watching through field glasses. When the balloon came down a couple of miles away, he turned to one of its inventors, Étienne Montgolfier, and said, "Magnifique! But now we must find out if the animals survived."

They had. And they proved to be in excellent condition. In a letter to his wife that evening, a triumphant Étienne playfully quoted the three as saying, "We feel fine. We've landed safely despite the wind. It's given us an appetite."

"That is all we could gather from the talk of the three animals," Étienne continued, "seeing that we had neglected to teach them French, one could say only 'Quack, Quack;' the other, 'Cocka-a-doodle-do;' and the third, no doubt a member of the Lamb family, replied only 'Baa' to all our questions."

Earlier, when the choice of animals was discussed,

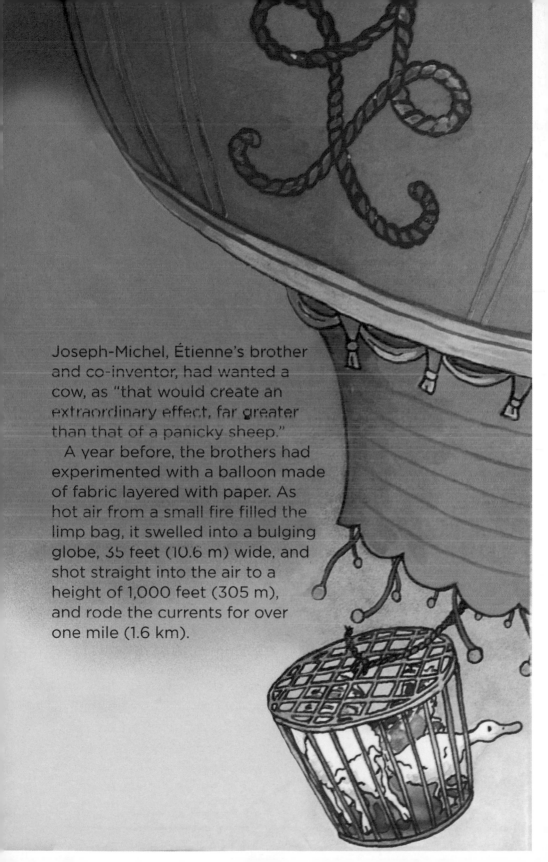

Joseph-Michel, Étienne's brother and co-inventor, had wanted a cow, as "that would create an extraordinary effect, far greater than that of a panicky sheep."

A year before, the brothers had experimented with a balloon made of fabric layered with paper. As hot air from a small fire filled the limp bag, it swelled into a bulging globe, 35 feet (10.6 m) wide, and shot straight into the air to a height of 1,000 feet (305 m), and rode the currents for over one mile (1.6 km).

The Russian government issued an airmail stamp honoring the contribution of Laika to its space program.

Thus was born the hot-air balloon.

After the successful flight of the sheep, duck, and rooster, it was time for the first manned flight in a Montgolfier balloon. It took place in Paris. One of the spectators was Benjamin Franklin, America's ambassador. When someone turned to him and said, "Oh, what use is a balloon?" Franklin replied, "Sir, of what use is a newborn baby?"

Find Out More

READ: *Feathers, Flaps, & Flops: Fabulous Early Fliers* by Bo Zaunders, illustrated by Roxie Munro

VISIT: space.com/16595-montgolfiers-first-balloon-flight.html

WATCH: youtube.com/watch?v=xYfjdSHQJOA

Eight Toxic Armpits?

BY HEATHER L. MONTGOMERY

Daddy longlegs are the spiders we run across the most often, right? Think again.

How many body parts does a spider have? Two. A "head" (called a cephalothorax) and an abdomen (where that sticky silk comes from). How many body parts does a daddy longlegs have? One.

So, these animals aren't even spiders. Daddy longlegs are one of many animals called opilionids (oo-pill-ee-OH-nidz). They are in the same animal class as spiders (Arachnida), and they all have long legs so they look like spiders—but they're a separate order.

Opilionids aren't dangerous to humans, but their predators had better watch out. Scientist Dr. Thomas Eisner discovered that a daddy longlegs carries toxin in its armpits. His research began one day when traveling through Texas. He picked up a daddy

Daddy longlegs have been around a very long time. It is believed that they split off from scorpions about 435 million years ago—about 200 million years before dinosaurs appeared!

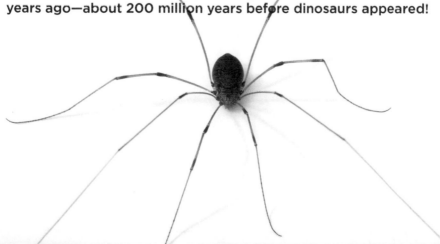

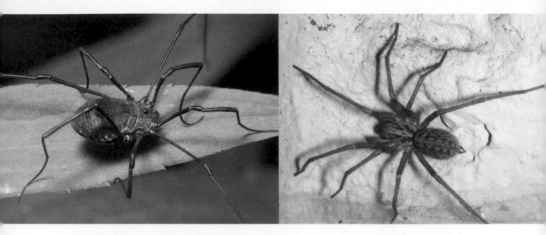

Left: Opiliones (*Hadrobunus grandis*) showing its body structure, single pair of eyes, and long legs. Right: This common house spider has two distinctive body parts and multiple eyes.

longlegs and smelled it. That's right, his nose was his scientific instrument. He observed an odd smell so he carted the creature back to his motel room and studied it. The smell was a toxic chemical called benzoquinone (BEN-zo-qwi-NO-ne). Of course, Dr. Eisner wanted to know more about that!

The chemical is toxic when it is a gas or a liquid, but not when it is a solid. On the side of the animal's body—basically in its armpit—Dr. Eisner found a sac-like gland. In that gland? Solid benzoquinone.

When a predator, such as an ant, threatens the daddy longlegs, it spits up a drop of gut juice. That liquid travels down a groove from its mouth to the gland. In less than a second, the daddy longlegs dissolves a bit of that benzoquinone into the liquid and creates toxic ammunition. You know those two long legs daddy longlegs use as feelers? He dips the tip of one of them into the toxic drop then slaps it on his predator. Take that, you scary ant!

The opilionid can reload its feelers up to thirty times from one toxic drop. When its ammo runs low, all it needs to do is drink water and spit again. Other types of opilionids skip the feelers and just let the liquid ooze out around their body, creating a super-toxic safety shield.

What other secrets might opilionids be hiding? Not many people study them, so who knows? Maybe you will sniff out a discovery!

Find Out More

READ: *Harvestmen: Secret Operatives* (Arachnid World) by Sandra Markle

VISIT: mentalfloss.com/article/59455/15-fascinating-facts-about-daddy-longlegs

WATCH: youtube.com/watch?v=aiJd2DHjJ5A
livescience.com/33625-daddy-longlegs-spiders-poisonous.html

Below, an opilionid spits up gut juice (A), mixes in toxic chemicals (B), dabs the tip of a feeler in it (C), and slaps the toxic liquid on the tweezers (D).

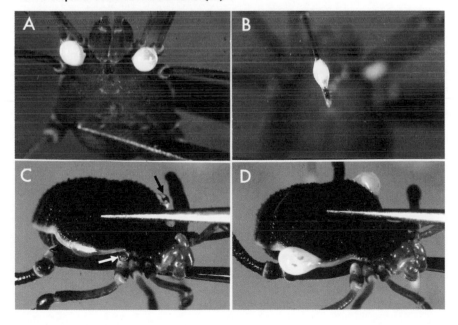

The grey wolf has always been feared by humans and has probably been persecuted more than any other animal. Wolves were the first animals to be placed on the US Endangered Species Act list in 1973.

What's It Like Being a Wolf?

BY DOROTHY HINSHAW PATENT

Have you ever wondered what it would be like to be a wolf? You're born in a cozy, dark den under the ground, probably along with at least one brother or sister. Your eyes are closed shut, but you can smell and feel your way over to your mother to drink sweet, warm milk from her teats. Your father and older brothers and sisters bring food from their hunts to feed your mother.

Your eyes open in about two weeks, but you can't

Wolves usually produce four to six puppies in a litter.

**Wolves are known to roam large distances, perhaps 12 miles
(19 km) in a single day.**

see much in the darkness of the den. You nap a lot,
snuggled up to your siblings and your mom. Then,
about a week later, your mother leads you all out of
the den into the sunshine. How different it is up here!
Now you explore the wild world, wandering among
the trees, lapping water from a creek, wrestling and
tumbling with your brothers and sisters.

After you get bigger and stronger, you and your
family leave the den and move to a safe outdoor area.
It's scary at first, being in a strange new place with
no dark den for comfort. An older brother or sister

watches over you and the other pups while the rest of the family, or pack, goes hunting. When the hunters return, you rush up and lick their faces, and they share the meat they got on the hunt. The older wolves in the pack let you climb all over them and nip their ears and tails while they take care of you, protecting you from danger.

All that good meat helps you grow into a big, strong wolf, with thick, shiny fur. In the fall, you go along on

Born in late April or early May, wolf puppies grow up fast and reach their adult size by the end of their first winter. They are grown up by the time they are two years old.

The family-loving wolf has often been portrayed as a villain in children's literature. This illustration by William Holbrook Beard shows Little Red Riding Hood encountering the wolf.

the hunt and learn how to find game and how best to catch it. Hunting is exciting but dangerous. You or other family members might get kicked by a deer or stomped on by a moose. But if you get injured, the other wolves take care of you until you recover. You are family, and family is what matters.

Find Out More

READ: *Wolves* by Seymour Simon

VISIT: wolf.org

WATCH: youtube.com/watch?v=ZMuMIcQx9Qc

Did the Hero Dog Survive?

BY LAURENCE PRINGLE

In 1804, US President Thomas Jefferson sent Meriwether Lewis, William Clark, and a team of men on a vital mission to explore the wild, unmapped West.

Lewis brought his dog along. According to journals kept by several of the explorers, the dog helped a lot. He retrieved animals that had been shot for food. He scared away grizzly bears and a bull bison that charged into camp.

The Lewis and Clark Expedition was the first American expedition to cross what is now the western portion of the United States, departing in May 1804, from near St. Louis on the Mississippi River. Seaman was along on every bit of the round-trip expedition of over 7,000 miles (11,200 km).

FORT CLATSOP
COLUMBIA RIVER
BLACKFEET
GREAT FALLS
NEZ PERCE
THREE FORKS
SHOSHONE
SNAKE RIVER
FORT MANDAN
SIOUX
DEATH OF
SGT. FLOYD
boundary not determined
PITTSBURGH
PHILADELPHIA
WASHINGTON D.C.
SAINT
CHARLES
CAMP WOOD
ST. LOUIS
SPANISH
TERRITORY
LOUISIANA
ACQUIRED BY THE US IN 1803
UNITED
STATES

**LEWIS AND CLARK
EXPEDITION
1804-1806**

Statue of Seaman accompanied by William Clark (left) and Meriwether Lewis (right) outside the Lewis and Clark Interpretive Center in Sioux City, Iowa.

"Spirit of Discovery"
by Pat Kennedy
2002

Commissioned by
Missouri River Historical Development, Inc.

Art Consultant: Steven Boody

The old journal pages are often hard to read, and this led to a misunderstanding of the dog's name. People thought that he was called Scannon. Not until 1985 did a historian carefully examine every mention of the dog. He found that Lewis had actually named the dog Seaman. The dog was a Newfoundland, a breed often kept on ships. They were great swimmers and could save people from drowning.

In the expedition's journals, Seaman was last mentioned in July 1806, two months before the explorers returned from the West and reached the little town of St. Louis on the Mississippi River. After that, there is no word about the dog in letters or reports written by Lewis, Clark, or others.

The mystery of what happened to Seaman was solved in the year 2000, thanks to the work of historian James Holmberg. He had found a book, written in 1814 by educator Timothy Alden, which told of a little museum in Virginia. Alden found a dog collar displayed there that William Clark had given to the museum. On the collar were these words: "The greatest traveller of my species. My name is SEAMAN, the dog of captain Meriwether Lewis, whom I accompanied to the Pacifick ocean through the interior of the continent of North America."

The collar was later destroyed by fire, but in his 1814 book, Timothy Alden also wrote further details about Seaman. Historians report that after the expedition, Meriwether Lewis' life became one of failure and despair. In October 1809, he took his own life. Alden wrote that Seaman was there when Lewis was buried, and "refused to take every kind of food, which was offered to him, and actually pined away and died with grief upon his master's grave."

People who know Newfoundland dogs say that this could be true because these dogs are fiercely loyal

Portraits of William Clark (left) and Meriwether Lewis (right) by Charles Willson Peale.

to their owners. Unless historians find some new evidence, that is how the life of this great dog hero ended.

Find Out More

READ: *Dog of Discovery: A Newfoundland's Adventures with Lewis and Clark* by Laurence Pringle

VISIT: lewisandclark.org/wpo/pdf/vol11no3.pdf

WATCH: youtube.com/watch?v=fCMWqdqHvH8

Ants in a Jam

BY SARAH ALBEE

Everyone hates getting stuck in traffic. Sometimes there are just too many cars trying to get where they're going and not enough space for them to maneuver. Did you know there are scientists who study traffic jams? These scientists have been looking at ways to help drivers reduce traffic bottlenecks and avoid collisions. Where do these scientists turn for problem-solving help? They observe ants.

There are trillions of ants on the planet, and most ants do a lot of commuting to and from the nest in search of food. But unlike human commuters, ants don't get jammed up. Ants on their way out of the nest make way for inbound ants carrying loads of food. Inbound ants get the center lane. Outbound ants move either to the right or to the left.

Leaf-cutter ants at work.

Leaf-cutter ants can be serious agricultural pests. For example, the largest leaf-cutter species is capable of defoliating an entire citrus tree in less than 24 hours.

Leaf-cutter ants are especially helpful to observe. Leaf-cutters can be any of a number of species of ants equipped with powerful mandibles (jaws). They travel in long lines through the rainforest, leaving a scent along the trail to find their way back. After an ant saws a chunk out of a leaf, it flings it over its back and then joins the super-highway of nest-mates heading back to the nest. Once there, the ant's colleagues chew the vegetation into a pulp and then mix it with ant poop and fungus spores. The ants eat the resulting fungus that grows from the decomposed goop.

In one recent study, scientists blocked the path and created a narrow passageway between leaf-cutter ants and their nest to see what the ants would do. Not only did the ants at the front show the ants behind them an efficient route back to the nest, but the chain of ants also somehow communicated—ant by ant—the

Leaf-cutter ants are often recognized by the long lines they form while carrying their leafy booty. Such a line can be as long as 98 feet (30 m).

Leaf-cutter ants are capable of carrying more than twenty times their body weight.

need to carry a smaller piece of leaf to fit through the narrower passage the scientists had created.

None of them bumped into anything, even while lugging leaves ten times their body weight. By working together and adapting quickly, the ants communicated information and reinforced the trail using what scientists call "distributed intelligence."

Can cars communicate the same way?

In the not-very-distant future, we may all be tooling around in self-driving cars, but the technology isn't perfect yet. Scientists have been studying ant traffic patterns to help invent different systems where massive amounts of interacting units have to move around without crashing into one another. In addition to traffic jams, scientists are studying ways to apply ant-like ingenuity to fields of study, such as molecular biology, telecommunications, and yes, driverless cars.

Find Out More

READ: *Ants* by Melissa Stewart

VISIT: activewild.com/leafcutter-ant-facts-for-kids-and-adults/

WATCH: youtu.be/Xxnmh4lDYaU
ed.ted.com/featured/VR7dKcVX

Percy the Cat

BY ALINE ALEXANDER NEWMAN

Percy the coal black cat is a born wanderer. The former barn cat sleeps by the woodstove in winter, but in summer, he leaves after breakfast and stays out all night. For years, his owners, Anne and Yale Michael, never knew where he went. Then a friend called to tell them that Percy had made the front page of the local newspaper.

The Michaels live in Scarborough, North Yorkshire, in the United Kingdom, a seaside town on the Atlantic coast. Tourists flock there to visit the beach and ride the miniature train that runs along it. According to the newspaper, Percy was also riding the rails!

Percy's owners thought that he was just an average ordinary cat that liked to wander a bit.

Percy raced from his home through the fields to catch his commuter train each morning.

"We were shocked," Yale says. "I wondered if it was really our cat." Because the frisky feline was always losing his collar and tags, no one knew who owned Percy or where he lived. But after their friend recognized him in that front-page newspaper article, radio and television stories followed. Percy became famous.

The train station is half a mile (0.8 km) from the Michaels' home. To get there, Percy has to walk down the alley beside their house and cross the neighbor's yard and a golf club parking lot (where he occasionally stops for meaty handouts). Finally, he trots over to the sea cliff and through some woods down to the railway. Once Percy arrives at the train station, he dozes on a mat the railway workers have laid out for him until he hears the train whistle. Then, every day, he boards the train, takes a seat, and rides to the Scarborough Sea Life Sanctuary. Perhaps the smell of fish drew him there originally, but that isn't why he visits now. The curious cat behaves like any human tourist and visits the marine sanctuary to view the exhibits. The penguins are his favorite. Percy might watch them strut about for half an hour, before he strolls into the office where aquarium workers have been welcoming him for years. When it's time to leave, the furry penguin watcher hops back on the train for the trip home.

The Michaels rode the tourist train once. "He got off, as we got on," says Yale. "We said, 'Hi, Percy.' He turned around and came to us," but only in greeting. Then their popular wandering pet continued on his independent way. Now that they know about his daytime adventures, they're waiting to hear what he does at night. Perhaps a local disco?

Find Out More

VISIT: purr-n-fur.org.uk/featuring/adv23b.html
WATCH: youtube.com/watch?v=UFPmmtqFj1U

Percy is just one of the crowd on the way to the penguin exhibit.

Attaching a message to a Signal Corps carrier pigeon, circa 1917-18.

A Pigeon Goes to War

BY CHERYL HARNESS

Picture this: It's October 1918, on a cold gray day in France's Argonne Forest. World War I has been going on for four hideous, deadly years. You and about 500 Americans are smack in the middle of a massive battle. You're running out of food and ammo. Shells are exploding all around you and some of them are American! Those guys don't know where you and your buddies are, trapped in a hillside valley, surrounded by enemy Germans!

How can Major Charles Whittlesey, the commander of this lost battalion, let those other Americans know where his unit is? They're cut off from the telegraph wires, so should he wave a flag? That'll just draw more enemy fire! Had the messengers he'd sent been shot or captured? How about homing pigeons? In this awful war, more than a 100,000 of them are used to carry battlefield messages. The major sends all but one of his

Major Charles Whittlesey

pigeons only to see them shot out of the sky. Finally, the desperate officer calls for his last pigeon, named Cher Ami, the French words for "dear friend."

A German carrier pigeon used for aerial reconnaissance.

Major Whittlesey scribbles out a message: "We are along the road parallel to 276.4. Our own artillery is dropping a barrage directly on us. For heaven's sake, stop it." He rolls the scrap of paper, stuffs it into the tiny silver canister attached to Cher Ami's leg, and sends him up and away. This pigeon has flown eleven successful missions. Will he make it now? He must!

The Germans fire.

Cher Ami falls! He's hit!

But he beats and flaps his wings, gains altitude, and flies 25 miles (40 km). Despite being blinded in one eye and shot in his bloodied breast, Cher Ami delivers the critical message, still attached to his leg, dangling by a bloody tendon. And 194 American soldiers are saved by their brave, dear, feathered friend. For his heroic service, Cher Ami was awarded France's highest medal, le Croix de guerre (the Cross of War).

In the months after the war ended, on November 11, 1918, oceanliners carried Cher Ami and many thousands of other veterans to America. He continued to be treated, but in the end, his injuries were too serious. Cher Ami died on June 13, 1919.

Left: Engineers of the 302nd Engineer Regiment repair a roadway over a trench. African American soldiers of the 92nd Infantry Division (Buffalo Soldiers) head into action in France's Argonne Forest during World War I.

Cher Ami, stuffed and on display in the Smithsonian Institution. He's shown without his tiny wooden leg, which was carved by a fellow veteran.

Back in the US, Major Whittlesey gave speeches about the war. He said nothing about any sorrow or awful memories, so no one knows just why he jumped off a ship to his death in the sea, late one night in November 1921. But the memory of soldiers' heroism and of one bird's stubborn courage will never die.

Find Out More

READ: *Fly, Cher Ami, Fly!: The Pigeon Who Saved the Lost Battalion* by Robert Burleigh, illustrated by Robert MacKenzie

VISIT: americanhistory.si.edu/collections/search/object/nmah_425415

worldwar1centennial.org/index.php/communicate/press-media/wwi-centennial-news/1210-cher-ami-the-pigeon-that-saved-the-lost-battalion.html

How Skunks Play Fair

BY LAURENCE PRINGLE

Are skunks aggressive, dangerous animals? Or are they peaceful animals that try to avoid trouble? Well, biologists who study skunks think of them this way: If life were a sport, skunks would be known for their strong defense and for playing fair.

Skunk stinkiness comes from a chemical weapon called musk. Foxes, weasels, and some other mammals also produce musk, but skunk musk is especially strong and long-lasting. Only skunks use musk to defend themselves from attack.

Skunks are really very nice, appealing animals if you understand how they operate.

Young skunks look like smaller adults with stocky bodies, stumpy legs, and bushy tails. They learn how to use their defensive stink sprays within the first few weeks of life.

Picture a skunk ambling along in the night, looking for food. It digs in the soil to find tasty earthworms and beetle grubs. The black and white fur that comes with just being a skunk sends a warning. This color pattern is unusual among mammals. It signals: "Beware—don't mess with me!"

Suppose a coyote or other predator ignores this first warning and steps toward the skunk. When a skunk feels threatened, it faces the danger. It raises its tail and tries to look as big as possible. It stamps its feet and clicks its teeth together. It may growl or hiss.

Oh, oh! Despite all of these warnings, the coyote growls and comes closer. Now the skunk gets really serious. It twists its body into a U-shape, so it can see the coyote and also aim its rear end toward it. The skunk's tail arches over its back, away from its rear— the final warning. This gives the skunk a clear shot, and also protects its own fur from the stinky musk. Skunks try to avoid smelling bad!

From two grape-sized glands, a skunk can spray musk as a fine mist or squirt a stream. It can squirt accurately for about 12 feet (3.7 m), and hit an attacking animal right in the face. The musk stings the predator's eyes and can blur its vision for a while. And it stinks! Animals hit with this musk learn to never bother a skunk again.

In cold weather, skunks often gather in communal dens. In warmer times, they usually find shelter above ground.

Skunks are so appealing that some people want to keep them as pets. The legality of keeping skunks as pets in the US varies by state, with it being illegal in a majority of them. In other countries, skunks are legal pets, but ownership is complicated, and special permits are required.

A skunk's glands store enough musk to fire a half dozen shots. They need a week or so to produce more. This is seldom a problem because a skunk sprays only when its life seems to be in danger. Some skunks go for months or even years without firing a shot. That's fine with them. Skunks want to avoid trouble and "play fair" with their many warnings.

Find Out More:

READ: *Skunks* by Sandra Markle

VISIT: kids.nationalgeographic.com/animals/skunk/#skunk-babies-walking.jpg

WATCH: youtu.be/VZwlKANA43w
youtu.be/0-4xNQuqZ1k

The Fish That Sees Red

BY STEVE JENKINS

Have you ever noticed how photographs of underwater scenes have a bluish tint? Sunlight is made up of a rainbow of colors, but when it enters the water, the reds and yellows in the light are filtered out. The blues and greens penetrate deeper into the water and give those watery scenes their peculiar cast. Because there is very little red light in the deep sea, most of the animals that live there have never evolved the ability to see the color red. This is why many deep-sea animals are red. In the depths of the ocean, a creature that can't be seen is safe from many predators.

There is an unusual fish that takes advantage of its fellow sea creatures' colorblindness. The stoplight loosejaw, a member of the dragonfish family, can

The loosejaw (also known as dragonfish) is a deep-sea predator that gets its name from the fact that its jaws seem to be hinged in several places, so that they can swing open and capture prey and swallow it whole.

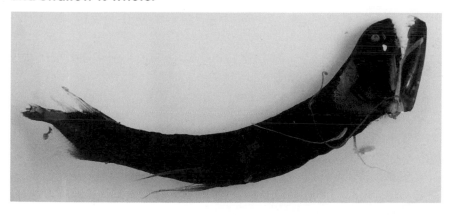

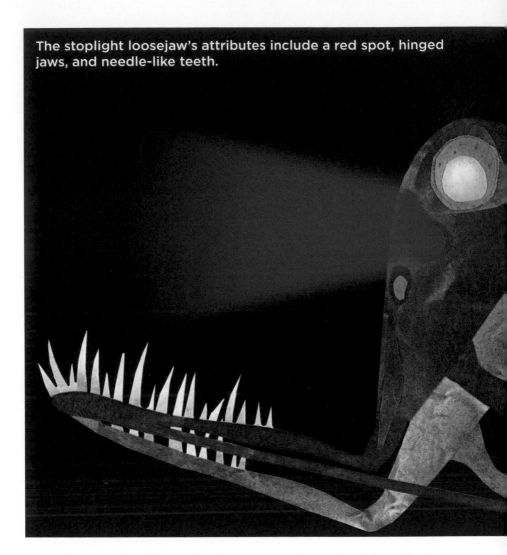

The stoplight loosejaw's attributes include a red spot, hinged jaws, and needle-like teeth.

see the color red. It also has a patch on its face that glows red as well as a glowing green spot on its face, which is probably used to communicate with other dragonfish. These red and green patches explain the "stoplight" part of this fish's name. The "loosejaw" comes from this fish's ability to open its mouth extra wide and swallow large prey. Scientists think that the open structure of the lower jaw allows the fish to close its mouth quickly, making it difficult for prey to escape. Relative to its size, the stoplight loosejaw has

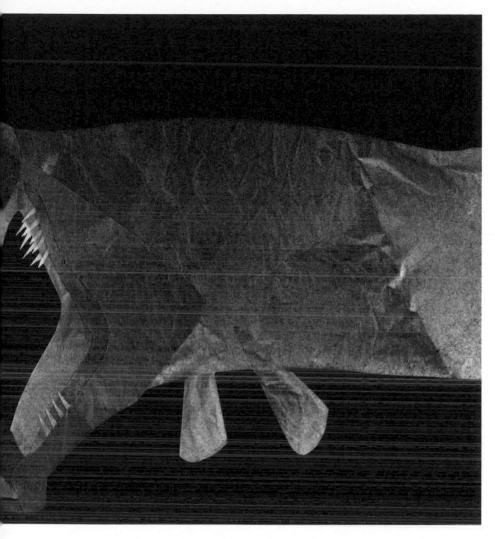

one of the widest gapes of any fish, with a lower jaw measuring one-quarter of the fish's length. It's not easy for animals that live in the dark waters of the deep sea to find prey. Many of them, including the stoplight loosejaw, have large mouths and sharp fangs that help ensure that their prey cannot escape.

Below about 650 feet (200 meters), very little sunlight penetrates the ocean. Below 3,300 feet (1,000 meters), the only light is that produced by living creatures. Almost all deep-sea creatures are

There are two kinds of stoplight loosejaws. The Northern (Malacosteus niger) shown here and the Southern. Together they are found everywhere in the world except the North and South Poles.

bioluminescent, or able to make their own light, but the light they produce is usually blue or green. When the stoplight loosejaw switches on its red spotlight, other creatures in the water are illuminated. Being blind to the color red, they don't realize that they've been spotted. Dragonfish are not known as picky eaters. If one of the lit-up animals is a fish, shrimp, or other suitable prey, the stoplight loosejaw quickly grabs it and swallows it.

Find Out More

VISIT: eol.org/pages/224918/details#life_history_and_behavior

WATCH: youtu.be/CukrrzfXvZg?t=11

Chimponaut: A Hero Forgotten & Remembered

BY JAN ADKINS

In 1961 the United States was losing the Space Race with the USSR. Its best rockets were blowing up on the launchpads.

On January 31, 1961, the US was ready to send its first astronaut into space on a long, high arc. He was only three feet (0.9 meters) tall. His name was Number 65. (If the rocket blew up, a "named" animal would sound bad in the news.) When asked by radio, 65 would press sequences of buttons on the flight control panel, then receive a banana pellet reward.

The blast off from Cape Canaveral (now Cape Kennedy) wasn't perfect. The Redstone rocket didn't blow up, but the launch damaged the passenger pod's hull. The controls didn't shut off on time and pushed

The chimp named Ham (primate Number 65) and a technician go over the equipment for Ham's suborbital flight.

Redstone launch with Ham aboard. Monkeys had been flown into space before, but Ham was the first higher primate to test a spacecraft.

the rocket much higher and much faster than planned. The chimp traveled at 5,800 miles (9,334 km) an hour, and reached a then-record high of 155 miles (250 km)! This put his reentry landing far beyond the US Navy ships sent to retrieve him. The pod splashed into the ocean, but water poured into the damaged pod. Number 65 was sinking! Two hours later, a helicopter picked up the passenger pod just in time.

Number 65 was a hero, so he was given a proper name: Ham. He appeared on the cover of magazines and newspapers as the United States' first man—er, chimp—in space!

In only a few months, human astronauts followed Ham's lead. Alan Shepard and John Glenn rocketed

This famous photo, known as the "handshake" welcome, shows Ham being welcomed back to Earth by the commander of the recovery ship, USS Donner.

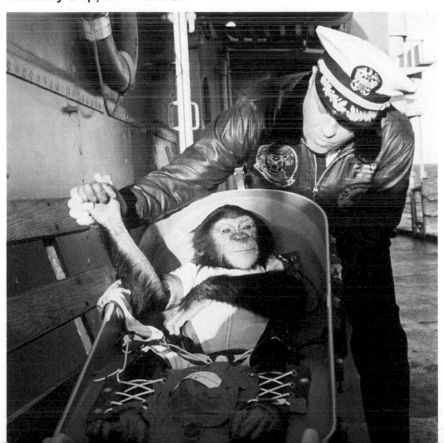

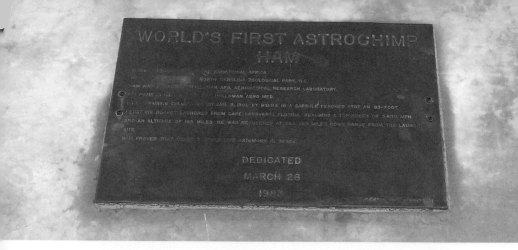

Ham's grave at the New Mexico Museum of Space History in Alamogordo, New Mexico.

into space and Ham was forgotten. He was given to the National Zoo in Washington, D.C., where he lived alone for seventeen years. He was trained as an astronaut and didn't get along with jungle animals. He often lay on his back and punched in imaginary button sequences as if he were still flying the capsule. The old chimponaut became lonely and depressed.

Ham was sent to a special "show animal" camp where he could reconnect with his wild brothers and sisters. He was taken to Andrews Air Force Base for the trip. As he was walked across the concrete, something wonderful happened. He passed between two lines of Air National Guard pilots, saluting Ham. Ham the brave Chimponaut finally got his honor parade.

Ham lived three happy years at the camp and died peacefully in 1983. You can see a plaque for Ham at the International Space Hall of Fame in New Mexico. It says: *"He proved that mankind could live and work in space."*

Find Out More

READ: *Ham the Astrochimp* by Richard Hilliard

WATCH: youtu.be/LIavbl0i5HQ

VISIT: airandspace.si.edu/stories/editorial/mercury-primate-capsule-and-ham-astrochimp

My Visit with the Penguins

BY JIM WHITING

Who doesn't like penguins? Their waddling gait is fun to watch. They have little fear of humans so it's easy to get close to them. Penguin movies, such as *Happy Feet* and *The Penguins of Madagascar*, are box-office hits.

I was fortunate to get up close and personal to thousands of penguins during a trip to Antarctica. As our ship neared the tip of the Antarctic Peninsula—the closest point to the southern tip of South America which had been our departure point—we marveled at how effortlessly they skimmed through the water

This photo was taken at the very tip of the Antarctic Peninsula, during the Antarctic summer, when temperatures often rise to just above freezing.

Adélie penguins have natural enemies, such as leopard seals and orcas, but their numbers are still increasing. A serious future threat is global warming, which melts the icebergs that are a major part of the penguins' habitat.

beside us. Soon we marveled at another characteristic. We were at least 2 or 3 miles (3 or 4 km) offshore when the harsh odor of the poop generated by all those penguins wafted over the ship.

We relished the opportunity to go ashore and wander through their rookeries. There were lots of juveniles, covered with gray fuzz that would eventually fall off

and be replaced by their characteristic black-and-white plumage. None of them seemed to mind our presence.

Despite this, we had several harsh reminders that we weren't in a zoo. Several century-old stone huts provided shelter for explorers who slaughtered hundreds of penguins to eat during the long, harsh Antarctic winters. Skuas, predatory birds, routinely

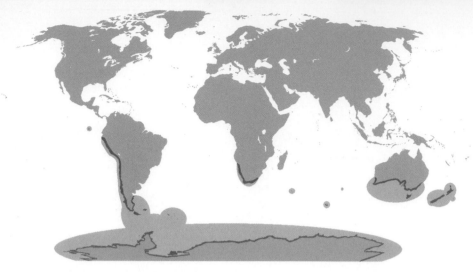

Although all penguin species are native to the Southern Hemisphere, they are not found only in cold climates, such as Antarctica. In fact, only a few species of penguin live so far south.

feed on penguin chicks. We saw the discarded remains of several skua meals. Danger can also come from the depths. A couple of times we observed large seals relaxing on ice floes with bright red stains next to them.

The saddest sight came one afternoon when we took a Zodiac inflatable boat to shore. A penguin stood

An emperor penguin in Antarctica jumps out of the water.

Both male and female penguin parents take care of their young for several months until the chicks are strong enough to hunt for food on their own.

Both penguin parents feed their chicks by eating fish, krill, or squid, digesting it or holding it in for a while. When the food is ready, the parent regurgitates it and then places it into the baby penguin's mouth.

forlornly on top of a small ice floe, a leopard seal thrashing the water next to it. We asked our guide if we could rescue the doomed bird. He shook his head. "The water is too rough," he said. "Too much chance of falling in if anyone tried to step out onto the floe. And you don't want to be anywhere near an angry half-ton (.45-metric ton) leopard seal that feels his dinner is being taken away from him."

On our way back to the ship, there was no sign of the lone penguin. We had to accept that we couldn't interfere in the natural course of things.

Find Out More

READ: *Penguins* by Seymour Simon

VISIT: antarctica.gov.au/about-antarctica/wildlife/animals/penguins/adelie-penguins

WATCH: youtu.be/ZOXQqT8tuVc

Lonesome George: The Face of Extinction

BY DOROTHY HINSHAW PATENT

*"Whatever happens to this single animal,
let him always remind us that the fate of all living
things on Earth is in human hands."*

These words—inscribed on a panel by the enclosure where the last of his race, the Pinta Island tortoise called Lonesome George—are no longer needed. George died on June 24, 2012, at an undetermined age. He was likely more than 100 years old. Even so, his actual death is merely a symbol of extinction because he was the only one of his kind left. Without a mate for George, this species was doomed.

It is said that George's head was used as an inspiration for the design of the movie character E.T.

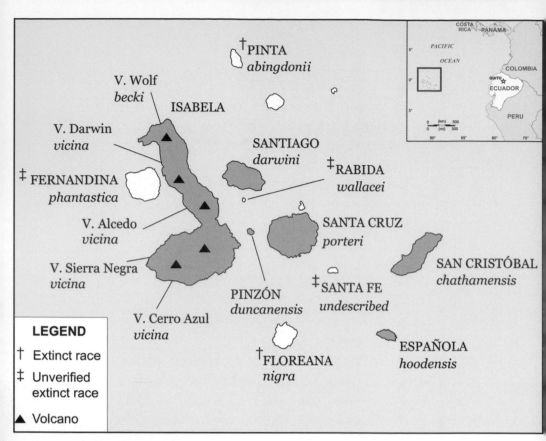

This map shows the current and extinct species distribution of the Galápagos tortoise by its subspecies.

Perhaps George's death will impress people with the power of our own species to doom or to save others. The thoughtless short-term thinking so common among humans ignores the longterm effects of our actions. During the 1800s, whalers, fur sealers, and other seafaring folks raided Equador's Galápagos Islands for food. The giant land tortoises that populated the islands were perfect for long-term storage, as they could survive for a year or more on a ship without eating or drinking. Their dilute urine provided drinking water as well. The Pinta tortoise population was hit the hardest by this exploitation because Pinta is the farthest north of the islands and thus the last one visited when the sailors left for the open sea.

By 1959, the tortoises had just about disappeared

from Pinta. Some fishermen released three goats there, knowing they would reproduce to make island meat once more available to ships. The goat population exploded, devastating the island vegetation and dooming any animals that depended on it for survival.

In 1979, a scientist studying snails came across George, who was soon brought to the Tortoise Center on nearby Santa Cruz Island for protection. But hopes of finding a mate for George and thus saving his species faded with the years, and Lonesome George became what he remains after his death: a symbol of careless exploitation by humans.

Lonesome George was on view in New York City's American Museum of Natural History from 2014 to 2015.

Scientists record information about the tortoises in their native environment. Unlike the Pinta subspecies, conservationists helped bring back the tortoises on the Galápagos island of Española from a low of only 16 to a population of more than 1,000 now living on their home island.

The American Museum of Natural History in New York did a careful restoration of George's remains, for a 2014-15 exhibit, after which he was returned to Ecuador. The plaque overlooking his old corral now reads:

*"We promise to tell your story and
to share your conservation message."*

Find Out More

READ: *Galápagos George* by Jean Craighead George, illustrated by Wendell Minor

VISIT: www.galapagos.org/conservation/conservation/project-areas/ecosystem-restoration/tortoise-restoration/

WATCH: youtube.com/watch?v=AZKbO2B7po0
youtube.com/watch?time_continue=21&v=MPPThxF2E9Q

White House Friends with Fur and Feather

BY CHERYL HARNESS

You know that presidential humans have lived in the White House since 1800, but so have many presidential pets, especially dogs. From those owned by John and Abigail Adams to Franklin D. Roosevelt's Scottie, Fala, to Bo and Sunny, the Portuguese Water Spaniels who live with President Obama's family, there have been many presidential pooches. President Clinton's daughter, Chelsea, had Socks the cat, but really, there haven't been as many cats in the White House. What about other kinds of pets?

John F. Kennedy's daughter Caroline had Macaroni, the pony. Willie and Tad Lincoln loved to hitch up their pet goats, Nanny and Nanko, to a cart or even kitchen

President Woodrow Wilson's sheep enjoying the White House grass (1919).

There is no doubt that the Kennedys were dog lovers. President John F. Kennedy and family, with Pushinka's puppies Blackie and White Tips, and family dogs Shannon, Clipper, Wolfie, and Charlie (Hyannis Port, August 14, 1963).

chairs and go banging and bumping through the White House! Thomas Jefferson had pet mockingbirds. James and Dolley Madison kept a parrot. So did Andrew Jackson, but his cussed and swore horribly! President Taft's pet cow Pauline Wayne and Old Ike, one of Woodrow Wilson's sheep, grazed on the White House lawn. Among Calvin Coolidge's many pets were Rebecca, the raccoon, and a goose named Enoch.

When Theodore Roosevelt became president in 1901, things really got lively, inside and outside the White House. He and his wife had six children and—boy, oh boy—did they have pets! In addition to plenty of horses, dogs, and a couple of cats, there was a lizard, a pig, a rabbit, a rat, one small bear, five guinea pigs, a macaw, an owl, a one-legged rooster, and Josiah, a badger. Alice, the oldest daughter, loved startling people by taking Emily Spinach out of her handbag. (Emily was a green snake, named after a skinny aunt.)

Clockwise from top left: Algonquin the pony for President Teddy Roosevelt's son Quentin. Theodore Jr., son of President Theodore Roosevelt, with his macaw, Eli. President Herbert Hoover's opossum, called Billy Possum. President Warren Harding named his pet squirrel, Pete. First Lady Grace Coolidge shows off her pet raccoon, Rebecca

President Obama enjoying Bo, one of the family's two Portuguese Water Dogs.

One day, Archie Roosevelt, one of Alice's little brothers, was sick upstairs. Two of her other brothers, Quentin and Kermit, got their Shetland pony, Algonquin, into the White House elevator and up they went to visit Archie. As his dad, President Roosevelt, would say, Archie was "deee-lighted!" Visiting pets didn't go over quite so well when little Quentin interrupted an Oval Office meeting and accidentally dropped the four snakes he had brought to show his dad!

Oh yes, it can be difficult being the president. Long, long ago, President Harry Truman said, "If you want a friend in Washington, get a dog." Remember that, if you ever get elected. And when you move to the White House, don't forget to bring your pet!

Find Out More

READ: *Presidential Pets: The Weird, Wacky, Little, Big, Scary, Strange Animals That Have Lived in the White House* by Julia Moberg, illustrated by Jeff Albrecht Studios

VISIT: presidentialpetmuseum.com

WATCH: cnn.com/2012/05/14/politics/presidential-pets /index.html

Taz in Big Trouble

BY LAURENCE PRINGLE

A lot of people are fond of the cartoon character called Taz. He is loud, always hungry, not very smart, and sometimes spins his body around like a little tornado. He pops up in video games and even appears in television ads.

Cartoon Taz is based on a real animal known as a Tasmanian devil. The "devils" are marsupials related to kangaroos and wombats. They used to live in many parts of Australia, but now survive only on Tasmania,

The Looney Tunes character Tasmanian Devil ("Taz") makes a personal appearance in a parade in California.

Young Tasmanian devils stay in their mother's pouch for 105 days, then remain in the family den for another three months. Only about three-fifths of them survive to maturity.

an Australian island state just south of the mainland.

Tasmanian devils have black fur and short legs and are about the size of a Beagle or a big house cat. Long ago, people named them "devils" because of the sounds they make. They grunt, huff, snarl, and click their teeth. They give out loud, fierce, blood-curdling screeches and screams.

And you know that spinning tornado thing that cartoon Taz does? It is based on the animal's actual behavior. When a Tasmanian devil is in a fight, or defending itself, it moves very rapidly. It flashes a view of its side, making itself look as big as possible. Then it quickly shows its front, with gaping mouth and teeth. Back and forth, back and forth it turns, showing two kinds of threats, and appearing to be whirling around.

Tasmanian devils fight a lot. They battle over food, and during mating season, males compete for females. This behavior has helped put their whole species in big trouble. Beginning in 1996, a disease began to kill the devils. It's a cancerous tumor that grows quickly on the faces of these mammals. When they fight, they often bite one another's face, spreading the disease. An infected animal soon dies. In less than 20 years, the Tasmanian devil population dropped by ninety percent.

Still, there is hope. Scientists have learned more

The Tasmanian devil generates a great deal of power in its bite—enough to tear meat and crush bones. The force is strong enough to bite through thick metal wire.

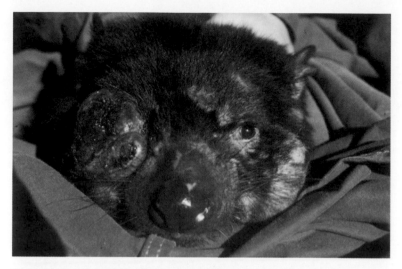

Tasmanian devil facial tumor disease causes tumors to form in and around the mouth, interfering with feeding and eventually leading to death by starvation.

about the disease, and perhaps a vaccine can be created to protect devils. Also, healthy devils are being kept in zoos and other places where the disease can't reach them. Scientists have learned that some wild devils in Tasmania seem able to resist the disease.

With help from people, Tasmanian devils may survive. We can hope these fascinating creatures make a comeback and once again scream loudly in the Tasmanian night.

Find Out More

READ: *Tasmanian Devils* by Sandra Markle

VISIT: parks.tas.gov.au/?base=387
animals.sandiegozoo.org/animals/tasmanian-devil

WATCH: nationalgeographic.com.au/videos/animal-encounters-with-ben-britton/ben-britton-tasmanian-devil-1626.aspx

The Bald Eagle Survives!

BY NANCY CASTALDO

The bald eagle population is an endangered species success story. When the bald eagle was selected as the US national bird in 1782, there were probably 100,000 nesting eagles in the United States. But by 1963, scientists counted only 487 pairs of bald eagles left in the lower 48 states. Illegal hunting, loss of habitat, and the use of DDT (a synthetic insecticide) had brought a beloved national symbol to the brink of extinction.

Even though bald eagles primarily eat fish and dead animals, many people believed that they preyed on

Using thermal convection currents, bald eagles can fly up to an altitude of 10,000 feet (3,000 m). When cruising, they can fly about 40 miles per hour (65 km/hr).

chickens and other domestic livestock. Many were shot needlessly. In 1940, US Congress passed the Bald Eagle Protection Act, which prohibited the birds from being killed. However, their population continued to decline because of a lack of nesting habitat. Bald eagles mate for life and return to their nesting territory each year for the rest of their lives. They live near bodies of water—marshes, rivers, and lakes—where they feed mostly on fish. Logging and development along waterways limited their nesting sites.

More than half of the bald eagle's diet is fish. The eagle swoops down and snatches its prey from the water with its talons. It also eats other birds and small mammals.

After World War II, DDT was a widely used pesticide against malaria-carrying mosquitoes and disease-carrying lice. Pesticides are chemicals used to kill or repel unwanted pests. Although it is estimated that many lives might have been saved by the use of DDT to kill dangerous pests, it was highly toxic to fish and other creatures.

Bald eagles and other birds ate DDT-contaminated fish. The DDT caused the eagles' eggshells to become so brittle that the eggs broke during incubation. The population of the US national bird declined to a dangerous low.

Rachel Carson's book *Silent Spring* brought the dangers of DDT to light. She wrote about how bird populations were suffering all across the country. Her book created an environmental movement that continues today. Lawsuits were filed in New York, Wisconsin, Michigan, and Washington D.C. to ban DDT.

Rachel Carson conducts marine biology research with national wildlife artist Bob Hines in the Atlantic (1952).

The bald eagle typically requires old-growth and mature stands of coniferous or hardwood trees for perching, roosting, and nesting.

Bald Eagles Mr. President and The First Lady reside at the US National Arboretum in Washington, D.C. Their activities have been streamed live for two years.

Scientific experts were gathered to testify and point out the dangers of the pesticide.

Ten years later all that hard work paid off. The pesticide was banned by the Environmental Protection Agency, and the eagle population began to soar again.

On June 28, 2007, bald eagles were removed from the list of threatened and endangered species. Success!

Find Out More

READ: *Beauty and the Beak: How Science, Technology, and a 3D-Printed Beak Rescued a Bald Eagle* by Deborah Lee Rose and Jane Veltkamp

VISIT: defenders.org/bald-eagle/basic-facts

WATCH: Live stream of Mr. President and The First Lady: youtube.com/watch?v=BsboWmgiOJY

Alex the Parrot, a Real Bird Brain

BY DOROTHY HINSHAW PATENT

The question "How smart are animals?" has puzzled many people for generations. Scientist Irene Pepperberg became intrigued with this question after viewing NOVA TV programs about communication studies in apes and dolphins. Trained as a chemist, Irene decided that her true passion was actually animal intelligence, not chemistry.

Irene plunged into learning what was already known about animals and explored the revolutionary ideas

Dr. Irene Pepperberg is a scientist noted for her studies in animal cognition, particularly in relation to parrots.

Irene asks Alex questions, such as, "What material is red and three-cornered?" The correct answer would be "leather."

of scientists who were changing how people thought about animals. In the early 1970s, people thought that animals didn't think and make decisions but merely responded moment by moment to their environments. Researchers working with apes and dolphins were overturning this concept, showing that animals could think, solve problems, and act intelligently.

What about birds, Irene wondered? She had kept pet parakeets and knew they were smart and could learn to speak at least a few words. She decided to study an African grey parrot, a popular pet that can learn to pronounce words especially well.

She bought a young parrot, named him Alex, and got to work. To probe Alex's mind, Irene needed to teach him to use words to describe his world. This took long, patient training. After a few years, Alex could name objects and foods, such as a key, a piece of wood, and a banana. He also learned several colors, and soon could label an object by both its label and color, such as "green key" and "yellow corn." He learned to distinguish whether an object was made of wood, paper, or rawhide, and could distinguish shapes, such as "three-corner" or "four-corner."

Alex also used his vocabulary to express his own desires. In the middle of an experimental session, he would say "Want nut," or "Wanna go shoulder."

As the years passed, Alex kept learning. If Irene presented him with a tray of items of different numbers and colors—say two green keys, four blue keys, and six red keys—he could correctly answer the question "What color four?"

By the time he died suddenly and unexpectedly in 2007, Alex had learned more than 100 labels and showed understanding of many concepts. When people asked Irene why Alex was special, she replied, "Because a bird with a brain the size of a shelled

The four blue cubes and balls and the four yellow cubes and balls didn't confuse Alex, who had learned to identify colors and shapes.

walnut could do the kinds of things that young children do. And that changed our perception of what we mean by 'bird brain.' It changed the way we think about animal thinking."

Irene continues studying the smarts of African grey parrots with birds Griffin and Athena.

Find Out More

READ: *Alex and Friends: Animal Talk, Animal Thinking* by Dorothy Hinshaw Patent, photographs by William Munoz

Alex & Me: How a Scientist and a Parrot Discovered a Hidden World of Animal Intelligence—and Formed a Deep Bond in the Process by Irene Pepperberg

VISIT: alexfoundation.org

WATCH: youtube.com/watch?v=cO6XuVlcEO4

youtube.com/watch?v=j-CAhALUBvk

Watch a Webmaster at Work

BY LAURENCE PRINGLE

This summer, you may be able to observe an amazing event in nature. You can watch a small animal build a structure much bigger than itself, using materials from inside its own body!

This is what happens when a spider spins a web. Inside a spider are glands that can produce seven different kinds of silk. The silk comes out of little spigots, called spinnerels, at the rear of the spider's body.

A strand of spider silk is stronger than a similar strand of steel, and spiders use this amazing material

An orb-weaving spider with a beetle caught in its web.

A classic circular form spider web.

in many ways. If they catch an insect, they may wrap it in silk to eat later. Female spiders enclose their eggs in a silken sac to protect them. Some spiders—almost always females—make webs that are death traps for insects.

Webs can be in the shape of funnels, sheets, or domes, but the best-known are called orb webs. From an orb web's center, lines of silk radiate out in all directions, like the spokes of a bicycle wheel. After building this basic structure, a spider goes around and around, laying ever-bigger circles of silk. Some of the silk threads have sticky glue to catch a moth or other prey. A spider can create this whole complex design in an hour or less.

When an orb web is complete, some kinds of spiders wait right in the center. Others hide at an edge of the web. Wherever the spider lies in wait, the builder keeps a front leg in touch with the web. Vibrations from the threads tell a spider whether prey has been caught.

Spiders often have to repair their webs, and some species routinely build a new one every day. And they recycle! They eat most of their old web. After digestion, it becomes brand new silk for the next construction job.

You may be able to watch a spider on the job. Look for webs in a field, park, or backyard. Keep an eye out for webs near doors, windows, or on a porch. The nighttime lights from such places attract night-flying insects, and spiders often build webs there. They may or may not be orb webs, but watching any kind of spider at work on its silken insect-trap can be fascinating fun.

Remember: The spider wants nothing to do with you. It is just trying to stay safe and catch some food.

Find Out More

READ: *Spiders! Strange and Wonderful* by Laurence Pringle

VISIT: pestproducts.com/spider-webs.htm#Tangled

WATCH: youtube.com/watch?v=4Y9K1H6Yn6o

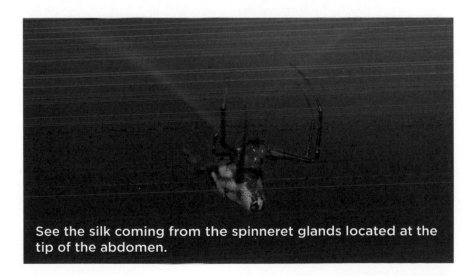

See the silk coming from the spinneret glands located at the tip of the abdomen.

Who Eats the Largest Jellyfish in the World— and Enjoys It?

BY STEPHEN SWINBURNE

Lion's mane jellyfish can grow seven feet (2 m) wide with tentacles reaching a length of 100 feet (30 m). That's the same length as a blue whale! Their bodies are ninety-eight percent seawater. They live in the cold, boreal waters of the Arctic, northern Atlantic and northern Pacific Oceans. Slowly pulsating ocean currents carry the big jellies great distances. The long trailing, stinging tentacles capture and tear apart their prey. Swimmers beware when currents sweep lion's manes close to shore. Their stings cause red swollen welts, and severe body contact with a lion's mane jellyfish may be deadly.

Lion's mane jellyfish with full threads visible

Unlike modern sea turtles, the leatherback sea turtle does not have a bony shell. This female leatherback is digging in the sand.

What animal can happily and safely slurp down a lion's mane jellyfish as if it were a big bowl of Jello™? The leatherback sea turtle!

Adult leatherbacks are the largest reptiles on earth today, averaging seven feet (2.1 m) long. As the planet's biggest turtle, they range from the Arctic Circle south to Antarctica, and they swim on average more than 6,000 miles (9,656 km) each year.

Leatherback sea turtles love lion's mane jellyfish. As a matter of fact, lion's mane jellyfish make up almost their entire diet. How can a seven-foot-long sea turtle consume a creature armored with 100 feet (30.5 m) of stinging tentacles?

Often referred to as Earth's last dinosaur, leatherback sea turtles have lived on the planet for millions of years, surviving ice ages and major extinctions. For an animal to live that long on a diet of giant blobs of gelatinous saltwater, it had better be very, very good at tackling and consuming its delicious but dangerous meals of giant stinging jellyfish. And, it better have developed some cool adaptations over the ages. Here's how they do it.

A leatherback turtle excretes salt from its eyes.

First off, a sharp, pointed lip acts like a hook so the turtle can snag the jellyfish and hang onto it.

Second, the turtle's mouthful of backward-pointing spines prevents the jellyfish from escaping. A scientist once said to me, while looking into the mouth of a leatherback, "It's the last thing a jellyfish will ever see!"

Once the leatherback has consumed dozens and dozens of jellyfish, there's the problem of all that salt in its diet. Eating too much salt causes dehydration. No problem for the leatherback! The turtle is perfectly adapted to rid its body of all that excess salt. Salt or lacrimal glands, located near their eyes, allow leatherbacks to secrete saline tears and then cry them away.

So the largest marine reptile on earth evolved by getting better and better at eating the most unlikely diet, the largest jellyfish on earth.

Find Out More

READ: *Sea Turtle Rescue: All About Sea Turtles and How to Save Them* by Karen Romano Young

VISIT: worldwildlife.org/species/leatherback-turtle

WATCH: https://vimeo.com/194042429

Leatherbacks are not the only turtles interested in the lion's mane jellyfish. Here, a green sea turtle is about to attack.

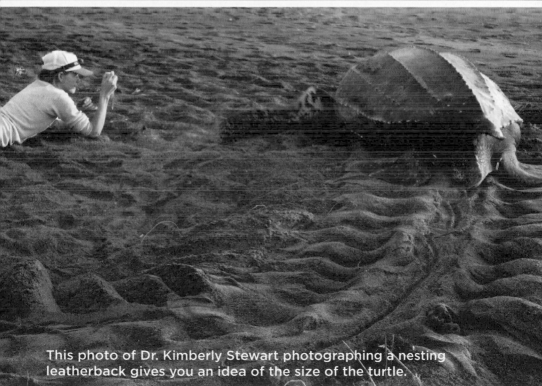

This photo of Dr. Kimberly Stewart photographing a nesting leatherback gives you an idea of the size of the turtle.

Everything Is Connected: The Butterfly Effect and the Wolf

BY DOROTHY HINSHAW PATENT

Have you heard about the "butterfly effect," the idea that one small change can bring about big changes over time? This idea is important in the study of ecology, which deals with the interactions of living things and their environments. Each element of an ecosystem has its place. When one element is eliminated, it affects everything else.

The Yellowstone ecosystem centered in Yellowstone National Park provides a great example. Late in the 20th century, biologists were worried about the aspen

These aspen shoots have been allowed to grow strong and tall.

This aspen shoot has been chewed to bits by elk.

trees there. Aspens occur in clusters that are actually clones growing from shared root systems. Some of the Yellowstone clones were hundreds of years old, but the old, dying trees weren't being replaced by strong young shoots. It looked like they might just die out,

Now that the aspens and willows are returning to the Yellowstone ecosystem, so are the beavers.

and no one was sure why.

When a severe drought in 1988 led to big wildfires in the park, the idea that fire might stimulate aspen growth proved wrong. Perhaps the elimination of wolves from the region in the early 20th century was to blame. Wolves? New trees? How could that be? Without wolves, the behavior of the Yellowstone elk had changed. No predators. No worry. So the elk became lazy, acting like cows, lying around in shaded areas along the rivers and creeks, munching contentedly on the juicy fresh growth of the willows and aspens.

In 1995, after much political battling, wolves were reintroduced into Yellowstone. The wolf population grew and the elk learned to be on the alert. As the wolves' favorite food, the elk had to change their behavior to survive—no more relaxing by a stream where wolves could easily sneak up and make a meal of them! They had to move around and spend more time in open places where watching for hungry wolves was far easier.

The wolves are changing the Yellowstone landscape in positive ways. The aspens and willows are coming back. Beavers, which had almost disappeared from some parts of the park, are returning. These rodents feed on aspens and willows and use them to build their dams and lodges. Beaver dams create ponds, and the ponds provide homes for hundreds of species of plants and animals, from algae and water striders to ducks and muskrats. The willows and aspen trees around the pond are nesting sites for songbirds and homes for insects and spiders . . . all thanks to the wolf.

Welcome back, wolves!

Find Out More

READ: *When the Wolves Returned: Restoring Nature's Balance in Yellowstone* by Dorothy Hinshaw Patent

VISIT: yellowstonepark.com/things-to-do/wildlife/wolves

WATCH: youtube.com/watch?v=L3BAg6eqqLE

Wolves on the hunt in Yellowstone National Park.

ABOUT THE AUTHORS

JAN ADKINS

Home base: Gainesville, FL
Email: j.adkins@verizon.net
Website: presently being rebuilt at janadkins.com

"All the good stories are real. How could we make up Vlad Dracula? Or Stephen Hawking?"

JAN ADKINS was a distracted, lackadaisical student and understands daydreamers in class. He has written and illustrated more than 40 books on widely different subjects, most of them nonfiction, and feels a special kinship with young readers.

For nine years, he was associate art director at *National Geographic Magazine*. He taught illustration at Rhode Island School of Design. He's a sailor and a cook, a hunter and a builder, and most of all, a delighted grandfather. He now hikes and bicycles and canoes around Gainesville, Florida.

You might enjoy Jan Adkin's trilogy—*What If You Met a Pirate, What If You Met a Knight,* and *What If You Met a Cowboy*. His latest book is *Bertha Takes a Drive*, about Bertha Benz taking the first road trip in the first automobile.

SARAH ALBEE

Home base: Watertown, CT
Email: albees@taftschool.org
Website: www.sarahalbeebooks.com

"My books are a mash-up of history and science. I believe high-interest topics presented with humor and passion can go a long way toward coaxing reluctant readers into appreciating history, science, and, yes, reading books."

SARAH ALBEE is the *New York Times* bestselling author of more than 100 books for kids, ranging from preschool through middle grade. She played basketball in college, and then a year of semi-professional women's basketball in Cairo, Egypt. Prior to being a full-time writer, Sarah worked at Children's Television Workshop (the producers of *Sesame Street*) for nine years. She lives in Connecticut with her husband, who is a high school history teacher and administrator, their three kids, and their dog, Rosie.

As a visiting author, Sarah helps kids make connections between their own lives and what happened in history. She also loves to help them with crafting their own writing.

Sarah's mission is to get kids to see how awesome history can be. She does this by choosing topics that interest and amuse them, for example *Poop Happened! A History of What People Do with Their Waste* or *Bugged: How Insects Changed History*.

NANCY CASTALDO

Home base: New York's Hudson Valley
Email: ntcastaldo@taconic.net
Website: nancycastaldo@nancycastaldo.com

"I write my books to inspire curiosity, empower my readers, and encourage them to think about something new."

NANCY CASTALDO spent her childhood climbing trees, exploring swamps, and searching under rocks. She studied science in school, and today Nancy writes about all sorts of science subjects, from polar bears to Russian seed banks. Along the way, Nancy has met detection dogs, researched endangered species, chatted with a bonobo, and met lots and lots of scientists.

As a visiting author, Nancy loves to engage students in research activities and empower them with ways that they can make a difference in our world.

Check out Nancy's recent titles: *Sniffer Dogs: How Dogs (and Their Noses) Save the World*, *Beastly Brains: Exploring How Animals Think, Talk, and Feel*, Green Earth Book Award title, *The Story of Seeds: From Mendel's Garden to Your Plate and How There's More of Less To Eat Around The World*, that delves into the history and future of our food. Her newest title is *Back from the Brink: Saving Animals from Extinction*, will show readers what we can accomplish when we all work together.

VICKI COBB

Home base: Greenburgh, NY
Email: email@vickicobb.com
Website: www.vickicobb.com
Blog: www.huffingtonpost.com/vicki-cobb

"All of my work is dedicated to giving the joy of discovery to children, which creates the foundation for a lifetime of ongoing inquiry and learning."

VICKI COBB, the "Julia Child" of kids' hands-on science, was born in New York City where she attended a private progressive school in Greenwich Village from kindergarten to sixth grade. When she went off to college, it wasn't nearly as much fun, but she did become very interested in science.

Her first jobs after graduating were in lab research. They involved doing the same things over and over again. So she went back to school to become a science teacher. Teaching was a blast! But, she decided that the thing she enjoyed most was writing science books for children. Looking back, after 90+ books, she realizes that she's made her life's work creating elementary school for herself so she would never stop having fun!

Vicki Cobb's classic book, *Science Experiments You Can Eat* was released bigger and better than ever in 2016. Her five most fun books that are quick bets about science are now in one huge book: *We Dare You!* You can see the videos at www.wedareyouvideos.com. You might also check out her DK biographies on Marie Curie and Harry Houdini.

CHERYL HARNESS

Home base: Independence, MO
Email: cheryl@cherylharness.com
Website: www.cherylharness.com

"I see my job as countering the notion that history consists of boring factoids about dead people and wars. No, it's a big, fat ongoing drama."

CHERYL HARNESS entered into the world at the time-space intersection of 1951—southern California, but it wasn't long before her restless parents moved back home to western Missouri. Having decided to take Cheryl along on this and lots of other moves, she grew up in a series of book-filled houses thereabouts, with a seemingly endless succession of younger siblings. She read and drew a lot, studied art at the University of Central Missouri and worked as a greeting card artist, unwittingly preparing herself to be an author and/or illustrator of about 50 books. She's talks a lot about them with school kids all over the country, and then goes home to Independence, Missouri, to be with her Shih Tzu, Mimi Squashface Barkymouth, and her cat, Kitty Boy. There's an awful lot to like, learn, and look at in Cheryl's historical picture books, like *Ghosts of the Civil War, The Remarkable Benjamin Franklin,* and *Remember the Ladies*. She illustrated all three of them.

Cheryl's lively biographies and social histories are noted for their detailed illustrations, researched in her travels round the nation.

STEVE JENKINS

Home Base: Boulder, CO
E-mail: www.stevejenkinsbooks.com
Website: steve@jenkinspage.com

"Children don't need anyone to give them a sense of wonder; they already have that. But they do need a way to incorporate the various bits and pieces of knowledge they acquire into some logical picture of the world. For me, science provides the most elegant and satisfying way to construct this picture."

 STEVE JENKINS was born in the mountains of North Carolina. His father, a physics professor, did research and taught at various universities. Steve planned to be a scientist himself, but at the last minute decided to go to art school in North Carolina, where he studied graphic design. After graduating he moved to New York City and worked in advertising and design, first in large firms and then with his wife, Robin Page, in their own design firm.

It was reading to his own three children that started Steve thinking about writing and illustrating books. For Steve, making books represents the happy intersection of children, science, art, his design partnership with his wife, and his lifelong love of reading.

To date, he has written and illustrated more than forty nonfiction picture books, including the Caldecott Honor–winning *What Do You Do with a Tail Like This?* and the Boston Globe Horn Book honor–winning *The Animal Book*. His most recent books are *Apex Predators: Top Killers Past and Present* and *Who Am I?*, an animal guessing game written with Robin Page.

TRISH MARX

Home base: New York City, NY

Email: trish.marx@gmail.com
Website: www.trishmarx.com

"In writing nonfiction for middle graders, I look for what wordlessly touches me. For a book about the mummies of southern Peru, the arrow connecting me to the rest of the story was the balls of yarn, still vibrantly red and yellow, found in the tomb of a thousand-year-old mummy. My grandmother's balls of yarn, in her knitting basket, looked just the same."

TRISH MARX was crazy for her dad's National Geographic magazines when she was a kid. She lived in a small but vibrant town in the great state of Minnesota surrounded by some of the world's richest farmlands. She loved her environment, but the magazines brought the big and varied world to her.

Trish attended University in St. Paul, Minnesota, and then 20 years later, after getting married and raising three children, she went back to school to earn a master's degree in Journalism from the University of Minnesota. Feeling equipped to see the world for herself at long last, she worked with photographer Cindy Karp traveling to Cuba, Kosovo, and the Middle east, eating meals, doing yoga, and sleeping on a borrowed cot in a tent with thirty refugees from the war in Kosovo.

Today she is recovering from a stroke. She lives in New York City and summers on a Maine Island where she helps bring books and reading to local children. She feeds her 40-year-old turtle, Marcus, video chats with her grandchild, and talks to a family of ravens every afternoon.

HEATHER L. MONTGOMERY

Home base: Ardmore, AL
Email: sipsey21@gmail.com
Website: HeatherLMontgomery.com

"Research is my life! A bug that throws his poop? Why?

Where? How? I just have to know."

HEATHER L. MONTGOMERY grew up climbing trees in the forest of eastern Virginia. She now lives in northern Alabama where she's still climbing trees. From a treetop, she can spy on a fox, experience a rainstorm as a bird would, and scribble furiously in her nature journal.

Snake tongues, spider silk, space quakes—these are a few of the inspirations for Heather's writing. Insects are her passion, but she's got questions about everything in nature: Whose skull is that? How does that worm shoot slime out of its face? Why is that poop purple? Answers off the internet just aren't good enough for her. Heather's got to get elbow-deep in her research topic even if it's blood and guts and goop.

When she is not writing, you can find Heather painting her face with mud, hiking into the wilderness, or catching critters in a creek.

A few of Heather's books include *Something Rotten: A Fresh Look at Roadkill; Bugs Don't Hug: Six-Legged Parents and Their Kids; How Rude: Real Bugs Who Won't Mind Their Manners; Rattlesnakes (Wild About Snakes);* and *Unsolved Mysteries of Nature.*

ROXIE MUNRO

Home base: New York, NY
E-mail: roxiesstudio@gmail.com
Website: www.roxiemunro.com

"Nonfiction is more exciting and stimulating than most fiction—we live in an amazing world."

ROXIE MUNRO grew up in southern Maryland, by the Chesapeake Bay. At six, she won first prize in a county-wide contest for a painting of a bowl of fruit, the start of a life-long career as an artist.

In 1980 she moved to New York City, when *The New Yorker* magazine started buying her paintings for covers; she's had fourteen published. In the mid-1980s, Roxie started writing and illustrating children's books. She's gone on to publish more than forty award-winning nonfiction books, and three interactive "Roxie" apps. Subjects include architecture, nature, biographies, and concepts, like quirky ABC books, mazes, lift-the-flap paper-engineered books, and more, many using "gamification" to engage children. She has also created giant kid-sized stage-set designs for KIWi (Kids Interactive Walk-In) Storybooks, as well as nine apps built to work with them. Roxie loves to take content crossmedia.

Rodent Rascals (2018) joins Roxie's nature book series on fascinating critters: *Hatch!* (birds), *Busy Builders* (bugs), and *Slithery Snakes.* They all use simple games or concepts to impart information. *EcoMazes: 12 Earth Adventures* and *Market Maze* use mazes to explain ecosystems and where our food comes from. She has a new book about art, called *Masterpiece Mix.*

ALINE ALEXANDER NEWMAN

Home base: Turin, New York
Email: aanewman@northnet.org
Website: www.alinealexandernewman.com

"Mercy to animals means mercy to humankind. Henry Bergh, founder of the American Society for the Prevention of Cruelty to Animals (ASPCA), believed that. And so do I. My hope is that my true stories of animals in action will inspire children to become believers, too."

ALINE ALEXANDER NEWMAN comes from a family of animal lovers. Her grandmother raised horses. One cousin kept a pet elephant and another helped Jane Goodall study wild chimpanzees. Aline's interest began with three blind

mice. When she was eight years old, she rescued the tiny orphans and fed them with an eye dropper.

As an adult, Aline became a Home Economics teacher, which is how she discovered her second love, freelance writing. Some 250 magazine articles, short stories, and newspaper columns have appeared under her name. It was her dozens of feature stories for *National Geographic Kids* magazine that eventually led to her writing animal books.

Aline and her husband, Neil, and their dog, Moose, divide their time between an old farmhouse in northern New York and a seasonal camp in the Adirondacks.

Aline's books include four titles in the National Geographic Kids Chapters series: *Ape Escapes, Animal Superstars* (Named on Amazon's list of Best Children's Books of 2013), *Lucky Leopards*, and R*ascally Rabbits*. Her newest book, *Cat Tales*, presents twenty three true stories of charming kitties doing amazing things.

DOROTHY HINSHAW PATENT

Home base: Missoula, MT
Email: doropatent@gmail.com
Website: dorothyhinshawpatent.com
Blog: dogwriterdorothy.com

"For me, the 'real' world of nature is the most fascinating topic possible. Who could invent the complex walnut-sized brain of an African grey parrot or the special odor-sensing cells on the feet of a butterfly? And the complex and beautiful relationships between humans and animals, such as that between people and horses, are equally intriguing. "

DOROTHY HINSHAW PATENT has always been fascinated by the natural world, growing up on the edge of the woods in Belvedere, CA. As a child, she loved riding horses and taking long walks with her Cocker Spaniel, Buffy, so it's no surprise that her books often feature dogs or horses and

how they interact with people.

After graduating from Stanford University, Dorothy received her PhD in zoology from the University of California, Berkeley. When she became a wife and mother, she puzzled about how to use her education and raise her family at the same time and realized she could translate her love of nature and books into books for young readers.

She loves sharing her excitement about animals and nature and about the relationships between people and the natural world with young people through her books and school visits.

Dorothy's most recent books include *Super Sniffers: Dog Detectives on the Job, The Call of the Osprey, Decorated Horses, Dog on Board: The True Story of Eclipse, the Bus Riding Dog*, and the upcoming book *Made for Each Other: Why Dogs and People Are Perfect Partners*.

LAURENCE PRINGLE

Home base: West Nyack, NY
email: octopushug@aol.com
Website: laurencepringle.com

"I am delighted to live in a nonfiction world and to be curious about much of it. There is such a bounty of fascinating facts, ideas, and discoveries. It can feel overwhelming—but never boring."

LAURENCE PRINGLE had a kind of free-range childhood in rural western New York. For a while he attended a one-room school. (That classroom had one teacher and about twenty kids in grades one to eight!) He loved reading and exploring woods, fields, ponds, and creeks. He wondered about the lives of birds, insects, trees, and turtles. He had so many questions! He did not realize he was laying a foundation for a distinguished writing career that would eventually total 120 nonfiction children's books.

Winner of several prestigious national awards, Larry has written for a wide range of grades over a wide range of subjects, including ecology, environmental and health issues, nature, history, biography. Although he freely admits that he is still trying to grow as a writer, he loves to visit schools to give programs about the writing process. Also, as a writer and reader, he is curious about why and how certain books were written, so his website features "the story behind the book" for many of his works.

Among Larry's favorites of his many titles are *An Extraordinary Life: The Story of a Monarch Butterfly*, *The Secret Life of the Red Fox*, *Ice! The Amazing History of the Ice Business*, and *The Secret Life of the Octopus*.

DAVID M. SCHWARTZ

Home base: Oakland, CA
Email: david@davidschwartz.com
Website: www.davidschwartz.com

"Children ask David why he likes math and science so much. That's like asking me why I like bones so much. For both, it's because they taste good."
                                   —*"Galileo" (you can call me "Leo")*

DAVID M. SCHWARTZ is a pretty good guy most of the time. He pets me, takes me for hikes, plays tug-of-war and he even reads to me when he wants to hear what his new books sound like—sort of like the children reading to dogs in this book. I guess you could say David loves me but that's not so special because he says he loves all animals—as if I'm no better than a razor-backed warthog.

David likes to wonder about many things and one of his favorite things to say to children is, "Wondering is wonderful." He says that his sense of wonder, including the questions he asked as a curious child, inspire his books. I wish they would inspire my next snack.

David's first book, *How Much Is a Million?*, has won all kinds of awards and millions of children have read it in many languages. *Where In the Wild?* is about camouflage, and it won an award for science picture book of the year. (I don't know how—there's not a single dog on its fold-out pages.) He has two alphabet books, one for math (*G is for Googol*) and one for science (*Q is for Quark*). All together, David has written 50 books. He says he'd like to write a million more. I'm not sure he'll have enough time because I need a lot of walks.

STEPHEN SWINBURNE

Home base: South Londonderry, VT
E-mail: stephen.swinburne@gmail.com
Website: www.steveswinburne.com

"As a life-long naturalist, I love sharing my passion for nature and exploring wild places. As an author, I love writing about wildlife and this amazing and beautiful planet we share."

STEPHEN SWINBURNE was born in London, England. When he was almost eight, he and his family moved from England to America. He's had many jobs in his life: newspaper delivery boy, dishwasher, busboy, waiter, pizza maker, truck driver, drummer in a rock band, park ranger, boat captain, and office worker. He's quite happy now writing children's books and will keep that job. His extensive travels have influenced his more than thirty books. Steve lives in Vermont with his wife, Heather, and loves to travel, read, sing, and play his ukulele.

Steve's curiosity and passion for animals can be found in many of his titles including, *Sea Turtle Scientist; Once a Wolf: How Wildlife Biologists Fought to Bring Back the Gray Wolf; Ocean Soup: Tide Pool Poems; Safe, Warm and Snug: How Animals Protect Their Babies; A Butterfly Grows; Black Bear: North America's Bear and Alligators Make the BEST Moms.*

JIM WHITING

Home base: Bainbridge Island, WA
Email: jimruns3@gmail.com
Website: www.jimwhiting.com

"Constantly learning new stuff is one of the main reasons why I keep writing. It's especially exciting to discover human details about cultural icons."

JIM WHITING's Terrific Tidbits:
1. He published *Northwest Runner*, voted by panels of professional journalists as the country's best regional running magazine, for 17 years.
2. He traveled to Antarctica to cover the Antarctica Marathon, although his most vivid memory of the experience is the smell produced by multitudes of pooping penguins.
3. He ran in both the original Olympic stadium, which dates back to 776 BCE (after which he was nearly tossed into the slammer) and the one erected for the revival of the Olympics in 1896.
4. A whale nearly rammed his sailboat *Rachel*. On the way back to the dock, he passed the *Pequod*, another sailboat. (If you've read *Moby Dick* you'll get the allusions.)
5. He's written nearly 180 nonfiction books for young readers, with another 60 or so in the pipeline. His goal: a stack of books taller than he is (one of the few times he's been glad he's short).

INDEX

Page numbers in **boldface** indicate an illustration.

PHOTO CREDITS

p. 7: ©Gecko gr/WC. p. 8: ©Cathy Keifer/SH. p. 9: ©AAP/Lukas Coch. p. 10: ©Valerius Geng/WC. p. 11: ©Shravans14/WC. p. 12: ©Hans Hillewaert/WC. p. 13: Audubon/WC p. 14: ©GUDKOV ANDREY/SH. p. 15: Smartse/SH. p. 16: ©Kelly L. Rogers/Johns Hopkins University Press. p. 17: ©Didier Descouens/WC. p. 18: Joelma Monteiro de Carvalho/WC. p. 19: ©gary powell/SH. p. 20 top. to bottom: ©Steve Heap/SH, ©nishikawa waranyu/ SH. p. 21: ©Rain0975/Flickr. p. 22: ©Tony Campbell/SH. p. 23: Nick Lothian. p. 24: ©Aline Alexander Newman. p. 25: ©huang jenhung/SH. p. 26-27: ©David Schwartz. p. 28-29: Courtesy of The Humane Society of Missouri. p. 30: ©Stuart Seeger/Flickr. p. 31: ©2013 Briscoe et al/PLOS. p. 32: ©keith ellwood/Flickr. p. 33: ©Charlesjsharp/WC. p. 34: ©Lina María Trujillo Mira/Flickr. p. 35: Dr. Christopher C. Austin et al/PLOS. p. 36: ©Dr. Christopher C. Austin. p. 38-40: WC. p. 41: LOC. p. 42: ©Fun Academy Motion Pictures. p. 43-44: ©Barbara Lavalle. p. 45: ©Sue Flood/Nature Picture Library. p. 46: ©Tambako The Jaguar/ Flickr. p. 47: ALAN SCHMIERER/WC. p. 48: ©User:Postdlf/WC. p. 49: WC. p. 50: ©Mark MacEwen/Nature Picture Library. p. 51: Prado Museum/WC. p. 52-53: ©Roxi Munro. p. 54: vintageprintable.swivelchairmedia.com. p. 55: ©Melinda Fawver/SH. p. 56 Left to right: ©Bruce Marlin/WC, Rob Mitchell/Flickr. p. 57: ©Reproduced with permission: Chemical defense of an opilionid (Acanthopachylus aculeatus), Thomas Eisner, Carmen Rossini, Andrés González, Maria Eisner, Journal of Experimental Biology 2004 207: 1313-1321. p. 58: ©William Muñoz. p. 59: ©Geoffrey Kuchera/SH. p. 60: ©Debbie Steinhausser/ SH. p. 61: ©William Muñoz. p. 62: WH Beard/LOC. p. 63: Victor van Werkhooven/WC. p. 64: Carol Highsmith/LOC. p. 66: CW Peale/WC. P. 67: ©SabineDeviche/WC. P. 71-73: ©Joe Coates, author of *Percy the Cat at North Bay Railway.* P. 74: WC. P. 75: NYPL.P. 76: LOC. P. 77: WC. p. 78: ©Jeff Tinsley/Smithsonian Institution/Publicresource.org. P. 79: USFWS Mountain-Prairie. P. 80: ©Bildagentur Zoonar GmbH/SH. P. 81: ©birdphotos.com. P. 82: ©qmnonic/Flickr. p. 83: ©Jamie Chang. p. 84: ©Seven Jenkins. p. 86: Emma Kissling/WC. p. 87-89: NASA. p. 90: ©Courtesy of New Mexico Museum of Space History, a division of the New Mexico Department of Cultural Affairs. p. 91: ©Jim Whiting. p. 92: ©ravas51/ WC. p. 94 top: Phoenix_B_1of3/WC. p. 94 bottom to p. 95: ©Christopher Michel/WC. p. 96: ©Indigo Images/SH. p. 97: ©farbled/SH. p. 98: ©Fallschirmjäger/WC. p. 99: ©RPBaiao/ SH. p. 100: ©Galapagos Tortoise Movement Ecology Programme/Flickr. p101: Harris & Ewing/LOC. p. 102: Cecil Stoughton/WC. p. 103 top. two: ©FB Benjamin/LOC. p. 103 all others: LOC. p. 104: Pete Souza/White House. p. 105: ©V Smoothe/WC. p. 106: ©KeresH/ WC. p. 107: ©Wayne McLean/WC. p. 108: ©Menna Jones/WC. p. 109: ©Steve Berardi/ WC. p. 110: ©Andy Morffew/WC. p. 112: USFWS. p. 113: ©Grendelkhan/WC. p. 114: © 2017 American Eagle Foundation (WWW.EAGLES.ORG). All Rights Reserved. p. 115: ©Jeffry Pike. p. 116-118: ©William Muñoz. p. 119: ©Fir0002/Flagstaffotos/WC: https:// www.gnu.org/licenses/old-licenses/fdl-1.2.en.html. p. 120: ©Stephencdickson/WC. p. 121: Hillebrand Steve/USFWS. p. 122: ©Derek Keats/Flickr. p. 123 top: USFWS. p. 124: ©Olivier Grunewald. p. 125 top to bottom: ©Rich Carey/SH, ©Claudia Lombard/USFWS. p. 127-130: ©Dan Hartman. p. 141 bottom: ©Sonya Sones.